MERCANTILISM

System or Expediency?

MERCANTILISM

System or Expediency?

EDITED WITH AN INTRODUCTION BY

Walter E. Minchinton

UNIVERSITY OF EXETER, ENGLAND

D. C. HEATH AND COMPANY
A DIVISION OF
RAYTHEON EDUCATION COMPANY
LEXINGTON, MASSACHUSETTS

Library of Congress Catalog Card Number: 69-19155

Printed in the United States of America

Table of Contents

Introduction

MERCANTILISM, system or expediency, has been the subject of a running debate among historians ever since the 1930's, when a fresh burst of controversy was sparked off by the publication of a two-volume study of *Mercantilism* by the distinguished Swedish economic historian Eli Heckscher. But the argument has a longer history. The term "mercantilism" came into the language of the English-speaking world in the second half of the nineteenth century following its acceptance in Germany, where writers like List and Gustav Schmoller employed it. In January 1888, *Harper's Magazine* spoke of "the mercantilism which succeeded . . . feudalism." Previously the phrase used in English had been "the mercantile system," a term earlier employed by Adam Smith to describe the economic thought and policy of the period between the end of the Middle Ages and the coming of laissez-faire. Until the 1930's writers in English tended to follow Smith rather than Schmoller, but Eli Heckscher's use of the word "mercantilism" gave it wider currency. But what does the word mean?

However employed, the term "mercantilism" is commonly used to refer to the whole range of economic thought and policy in the period between the eclipse of canonist views and the development of the classical theory of economics. During these years — the sixteenth, seventeenth, and eighteenth centuries — the situation in Europe changed. The discoveries brought Europe into contact with a wider world, there was a quickening of economic activity, and there was the emergence of strong national states which were anxious to use all the means at their disposal to strengthen their positions. To do so they needed to foster economic growth, to raise revenue, and to improve their administrative arrangements. Nor were they averse to waging war to achieve their ends. And in order to wage war, money was needed. According to Colbert, trade is the source of finance and finance is the nerve of war. Rooted in practice, mercantilist measures were those economic measures which would lead to the creation and maintenance of a strong nation state. "Mercantilism" can therefore be described as the striving after political power through economic means, which, given the circumstances of the time, meant through the encouragement of trade and manufactures rather than the improvement of the land. Such policies tended to be protectionist and monetary.

But can mercantilism be described as a coherent set of economic and social policies deliberately chosen and applied? Or were mercantilist policies a rag-bag of expedients which were employed willy-nilly as a result of the pressure of events and the activity of particular lobbies or interests? Was mercantilism an integrated theory, or was it a set of responses to a particular range of economic problems? Or to put the debate in a particular context: in the field of economic and social policy, were the Tudors in sixteenth-century England more forced than forceful? Is Tudor despotism myth or reality? In this volume are set out some of the varied ways in which historians have interpreted the term "mercantilism."

Before we consider what historians have said, let us first look, however, at two examples of divergent interpretations of thought and policy, both taken from the experience of England in the late sixteenth and early seventeenth centuries. For policy, the English Statute of Apprentices has been selected. Passed in 1563, this act was an attempt to deal with the depression in trade which followed the loss of the Antwerp market, the major outlet for the most important English export of the time, undressed woollen cloth which was sent to the continent to be dyed and finished. Because of European conditions and the absence of a market outside Europe, the sales of English cloth were drastically reduced. This shrinkage in demand had a serious effect on English foreign trade, on the cloth manufacturing industry, and on agriculture, which supplied the main raw material, wool. So in 1563 in a single session of Parliament fifteen acts were passed to control or encourage a wide range of economic activities. But attention has been focused on this single piece of legislation. Those who find some coherence in mercantilism have hailed the Statute of Artificers (or Apprentices)—like the French tariff of 1664—as a prime example of state economic activity. "It was," wrote Heckscher, "the most ambitious attempt in the whole history of mercantilism to define in a single law a national economic policy." While many other acts of the English parliament —the navigation acts, the iron act, the hat act, and so on—could have been printed here to illustrate mercantilist legislative activity, the 1563 act has been chosen because of Heckscher's claim. But this has not been accepted universally. Other historians, who see the economic and social policy of the early modern period as almost invariably the product of expediency, have argued that the 1563 act cannot be so described. In their view, it was not the embodiment of a coherent policy but a desperate measure, sponsored by the government as the result of the pressure of interested parties, to meet a period of acute depression. Not planning but desperation was its hallmark. And, they go on to point out, enforcement of the statute was secured more by the pressure

of those interests than by the government.

The Statute of Artificers is primarily concerned with internal economic conditions, but a major concern of many countries at this time was with the balance of trade. The views of mercantilist writers on this question changed in the course of time from a "bullionist" position, which held that the export of all bullion or coin ought to be banned, to one which recognized that such a policy was impracticable. These latter argued that trade policy should strive to ensure a "favorable" balance of trade. Of the numerous books and pamphlets which appeared discussing this question, one of the most influential was *England's Treasure by Foreign Trade: Or the Balance of Our Foreign Trade Is the Rule of Our Treasure,* by Thomas Mun, which Adam Smith said "had become a fundamental maxim in the political economy not of England alone but of all commercial countries." For some, therefore, Mun's book has been regarded as a straightforward contribution to economic thought but, as others have pointed out, it was not so conceived. Written in the 1620's, though not published until 1664 by Thomas Mun's son, it was a contribution to the debate about the trade depression of the 1620's and, like much other seventeenth-century polemical writing, reflected a particular interest. Mun himself was a director of the English East India Company, which came under frequent attack in the seventeenth century because its activities led to an outflow of bullion from England. Whether regarded as a contribution to economics or as special pleading in a particular debate, Mun's work is outstanding.

From the end of the seventeenth century, government control of economic policy, both internally and with respect to foreign trade, came under increasing criticism. With the changing economic position, with England poised for take-off into industrialization, the attacks grew to be summed up magisterially by Adam Smith in his *An Inquiry into the Nature and Causes of the Wealth of Nations,* published in the year of the American Revolution, 1776. Smith spent the whole of Book IV examining and criticising what he called the modern system of political economy, the mercantile system or system of commerce. Shortened though it is, as the extract printed below shows, Adam Smith required space to develop his argument. Almost without exception he wrote critically of commercial regulations and called for a reduction in the extent of national and local control of economic activity. In order to attack, Smith systematized and reduced to order — and to absurdity. He gave a false coherence to what had been discussed piecemeal and unrelatedly for a century or more. There were two main charges against the mercantile system made by Adam Smith and repeated by later commentators. First, a matter over which writers still argue, he alleged that the mercantilists falsely confused money with wealth and the favorable balance of trade with an annual balance of income over consumption. Second, he argued that mercantilism endeavored to secure this end by a conspiracy of merchants and manufacturers concerned not with the public good but with their own narrow advantage. Government interference was not evenhanded but partisan. The debate about the truth of these charges continues, but in his own time Adam Smith was successful. For a century or more the predominant strand of economic thought was critical of mercantilist ideas.

This, however, was not everywhere the case. Split into many states and principalities, the view gathered force in Germany in the course of the early nineteenth century that economic policy could contribute to political ends. As a result interest was renewed in the economic ideas and policies of the previous centuries. The relevance of such enquiries was made explicit by the publication of Gustav Schmoller's *The Mercantile System in Germany* in 1884. In a long historical disquisition he argued that economic policy could aid the establishment of a strong national state, that mercantilism was state-making. Schmoller's views influenced the writing of economic history not only in Germany but in other countries too. William Cunningham and William Ashley, two of the founders of economic history in England, both studied in Germany; and it was Ashley who was responsible for the publication of Schmoller's *The Mercantile System* in England in 1896 in a series in which Mun's *England's Treasure by Foreign Trade* also found a place.

More than a decade earlier, in 1882, William Cunningham had published his *Growth of English Industry and Commerce*, which reflected not only the influence of the German historical economists but also the nature of the historical sources most easily available in England, the records of the central government. Inevitably he saw the course of economic events from the standpoint of Whitehall and Westminster. In the section entitled "The Mercantile System," which deals with the sixteenth, seventeenth, and early eighteenth centuries, Cunningham devoted some attention to the means by which England, a previously underdeveloped area on the fringe of the international economy of late medieval Europe, brought herself nearer to the center of the world stage. The explanation he gave was in terms of a view of economic policy as power. "The rationale of the whole," he stated, "was the deliberate pursuit of national power." And when he came to discuss later Stuart England he drew a parallel with the France of Louis XIV and of his chief minister, Colbert, by entitling this particular section of his book, "Parliamentary Colbertism." Thus in changing their attitude to government economic policy from criticism to approbation, Schmoller and Cunningham added to Smith's comparatively limited concept of mercantilism as commercial policy, the notions of state-making and national power.

But Cunningham's views did not go unchallenged. Other English historians, among them W. A. S. Hewins and George Unwin, regarded government intervention in economic life as anathema. Neither of them wrote a sustained critique of mercan-

tilism, but each expressed his views pun-
gently and briefly. Hewins wrote of "the
restraints and prohibitions of the mercantile
system" with distaste and stated that "so far
as the erroneous principles of the mercantile system became the basis of a well-
defined policy, the results were disastrous."
But critical as he was of the notion, he still
employed the term "mercantile system" and
did not challenge the existence of this concept, as some later writers were to do. More
generally and more tersely, Unwin wrote,
"I think the part played by state power in
history has been largely evil."

This dispute remained unresolved, but
when the question of the nature of mercantilism once more became a lively question among historians the economic climate
had changed. With the First World War
the liberal dream faded, and though more
in America than elsewhere there were brash
espousals of laissez-faire, the stagnation of
world trade and the persistence of high
unemployment began to haunt men's
thoughts and to suggest to some the need
for a reconsideration of economic policy
and of the role of government in economic
life. But while there were some who wished
to see the sphere of governmental activity
enlarged, not all were of this mind. Among
the latter was the Swedish economic historian Eli Heckscher, who as an under-
graduate had written a study of the Swedish navigation act of 1721. A convinced
free-trade liberal, he embarked on a study
of mercantilism as a means of opposing
what he saw as the disturbing trend towards protectionism. In his two-volume
account which appeared in Swedish in
1931, in German in 1932, and in English in
1935, Heckscher defined mercantilism as
that phase of European economic experience whose chronological limits varied from
country to country as the course of economic development differed but which extended from the eclipse of the canonist
doctrine until the coming of laissez-faire.
He distinguished five characteristics of
mercantilism: the desire for unification, the
pursuit of power as an end, protectionism,

a monetary theory linked with the balance
of trade, and a conception of society. All
but the last had been identified by others:
the first by Schmoller, the second by Cunningham, and the third and fourth by
Adam Smith. It was Heckscher's achievement to bring them together and weld them
into a concept of society. In his book not
only did Heckscher attempt to bring coherence to an array of disparate elements;
he also tried to define the chronological
limits of the mercantilist era more firmly
and to place the discussion in a European
setting. But instead of acceptance, Heckscher's views were met with criticism, and
the publication of his wide-ranging study
led to a renewed debate about the nature
of mercantilism centering on his own
writings.

While they acclaimed his erudition and
his enormously illuminating analysis, the
majority of his academic colleagues in England and America were critical of Heckscher's system. In the climate of the 1930's
the prevailing view was that even if it
could be argued that some mercantilist
writers displayed a desire to make a scientific analysis of events as a guide to policy,
the majority used theory to justify and explain policies selected for other reasons.
Among the most critical commentaries on
Heckscher's work were those written by
Herbert Heaton and A. V. Judges.

Heaton's criticisms were wide-ranging
and caustically expressed. He felt dubious
about the shifting chronology of Heckscher's discussion and was critical of the
Swedish historian's view of the natural
economy of the Middle Ages. In the passage cited below, Heaton criticises Heckscher's notion of mercantilism as a unifying
force and comes to the conclusion that
mercantilism as a system of public finance
was vastly more important than considerations of unification. But Heaton is also
critical of the other aspects of mercantilism
described by Heckscher. On the second aspect, mercantilism as a system of power,
Heaton's views have much in common with
Viner's quoted below. Nor does he think

that mercantilism was so clearly a system of protectionism, since some of the export prohibitions were, he argues, revenue-raising rather than protectionist in intent. And he suggests more seriously that protectionism was a response to a changing economic system empirically adopted rather than a system abstractly applied. On mercantilism as a monetary system he restates the perennial controversy about this question. Last, he finds mercantilism as a concept of society unsatisfactory. Heckscher, Heaton argues, drew too much in his whole analysis on the writings of polemicists rather than on the experience of administrators and businessmen. In his exposition, he has failed to achieve the identification of situation, theory, and policy necessary to create an *ism.*

This is a point which Judges takes up at the beginning of his criticism of the idea of the mercantile state. One of the things we require of a system, he says, "is that it should be capable of systematic demonstration; while an *ism,* to be worthy of serious consideration, must offer a coherent doctrine or at least a handful of settled principles." This particular point seems less telling with the passage of time. Clearly, mercantilism is not an *ism* like socialism, or fascism, but is it not an *ism* like despotism or paternalism? Judges traces the history of the controversy through the eighteenth and nineteenth centuries and finally casts his vote against the notion of the mercantile state. But time has shown that the blow that Judges struck was less lethal than might have seemed at first. There is substance in many of the points he makes, but the usefulness of the term "mercantile system" or mercantilism to the historian remains. While he found some shortcomings in the term "industrial revolution," Professor T. S. Ashton declared that it had been used by a long line of historians and had become so firmly embedded in common speech that it would be pedantic to offer an alternative. Will it be the same with mercantilism?

While the controversy about Heckscher's *Mercantilism* continued, Heckscher himself was an active propagandist for his own cause. In the *Economic History Review* in 1935 he published an article in which he took the opportunity to restate his views. While he gave a little ground in relation to mercantilism as unification, he held firm on three of the other aspects — protection, money, and the conception of society — and held that the harmony of the system was clear. In only one important respect did he make concessions, rewriting Chapter 1 of Volume 2, which dealt with mercantilism as a system of power, to take account of Jacob Viner's argument on the question of power versus plenty. Viner argued that the two were not antagonistic but inseparable. Mercantilist writers, he averred, would have assented to four propositions: (1) that wealth was essential to power; (2) that power was essential to wealth; (3) that wealth and power were each proper ultimate ends of national policy; and (4) that there was a long-run harmony between these two ends.

Aside from this controversy a further contribution to the debate about mercantilism came from the pen of John Maynard Keynes, the English economist. In the course of his discussion of *The General Theory of Employment, Interest and Money,* which was published in 1936, he was led to attempt to rehabilitate mercantilist views. There he argued that the mercantilist notion that money, if not synonymous with wealth, was at any rate an essential ingredient in the wealth of the nation, and implied an intuitive recognition of the connection between plenty of money and low interest rates in stimulating investment.

Despite the critics, the term "mercantilism" as a word to describe the economic thought and policy of the early modern period, even if not as a concept of a coherent body of economic doctrine, gained currency. Among the scholars who found it useful was L. A. Harper, who used it to discuss a particular range of issues, the relationship between England and her American colonies in the eighteenth century. He concluded that "many of the misunderstandings which have arisen in connection with mercantilism and the American revolution have grown out of a failure to distinguish between the two phases of mercantilism: exploitation — in the sense of obtaining benefits from the colonies — and regulation." So, in a particular situation, Harper argued that "mercantilism was not unchanging but altered with the changing economic situation." And this is a point which can be validly made for other aspects of mercantilist thought and policy. He went on: "a large part of governmental activity consists in attempting to mould economic conduct and to minimise the friction which results from clashes and constraints. English mercantilism was such an attempt. It succeeded rather well in minimising friction until 1764. For the next decade it bungled badly, and the penalty was the loss of the Thirteen Colonies."

In his own writings Heckscher was concerned with the links between the age of mercantilism and the previous and succeeding periods, and these have been explored in more detail by later writers. In the course of a long article on "The Liberal Elements in English Mercantilism," William Grampp considered the doctrines of the mercantilists and argued that although these were derided by the classical economists, they greatly influenced their successors. It is ironical, he says, that English mercantilist doctrine should have been disparaged most by the men whose ideas it anticipated. A less enthusiastic view of the mercantilists was taken by Raymond de Roover, who found scholasticism superior to mercantilism because the former was part of a coherent system whereas the latter was a conglomerate of uncoordinated prescriptions. Scholasticism was eclipsed, he holds, because it attached undue importance to the question of usury, because it failed to discard the deadwood in order to preserve what was worth keeping. In their different ways these two articles link the economic thought of the sixteenth, seventeenth, and early eighteenth centuries with

the centuries before and after, and also contribute in some manner to the debate about the nature of mercantilism.

The reissue of Heckscher's *Mercantilism* in 1955 led to a further round of controversy but this did not in fact take the debate much further than the controversy of the 1930's had done. More constructive was Charles Wilson's discussion of "The Other Face of Mercantilism." In this article Wilson was concerned to extend the application of the term and to argue that social policy as well as economic policy was a matter of interest to the mercantilists, illustrating his point particularly from the standpoint of their concern about the question of poverty and poor relief.

While there continue to be scholars who would wish to abolish the word, in practice this has proved, as E. A. J. Johnson admitted in 1937, as difficult as it is to abolish sin. A countertendency of recent years has been to widen the scope of the term to embrace virtually all economic policies of the period between the end of the Middle Ages and the emergence of laissez-faire. Not all welcome this extension. There are those who would argue that the term should be reserved for matters of trade. Others, however, hold that the extension of the scope of the term "mercantilism" is justified since what, in their view, distinguishes the early modern period from the nineteenth century was the willingness of people in the earlier time to appeal to the state for help. Whereas to the men of the mid-nineteenth century, that government was best which governs least, to the mercantilists it was a right and proper thing for the state to intervene in economic and social life. Everything was thought possible to that strange thing, a government able to enforce obedience. While there are still historians who would eschew the term "mercantilism," there are others who would use it in a limited manner and yet others who would apply it more generally to economic thought and policy in the sixteenth, seventeenth, and eighteenth centuries.

Moreover, the word has gained new life

by being applied to certain aspects of the contemporary situation. When Joan Robinson gave her inaugural lecture as professor of economics in the University of Cambridge, England, in 1965 she entitled it "The New Mercantilism"; British restrictionist trade policy concerning the import of Indian cotton goods into Britain in the same year was called "bare-faced mercantilism"; while in America it has been said that concessions from the government — be they tariffs, quotas, or price supports — aid monopoly and have helped to create "the new mercantilism of the late twentieth century." The word "mercantilism" will continue to be employed because not only academic writers but also publicists, politicians, and journalists have found it useful. But the debate about the meaning of the word, which the following pages document, will go on.

[NOTE: Those statements quoted in the *Conflict of Opinion, pages* xv–xvi, by authors whose writings are not included in the text of this book, are taken from the following sources: E. A. J. Johnson, *Predecessors of Adam Smith. The Growth of British Economic Thought* (New York, 1936, reprinted in New York, 1960); G. N. Clark, *The Seventeenth Century* (London, 2nd ed. 1947); D. C. Coleman; "Eli Heckscher and the Ideas of Mercantilism," *Scandinavian Economic History Review,* V (1957).]

Conflict of Opinion

In its innermost kernel it [mercantilism] is nothing but state-making. . . . The essence of the system lies in the total transformation of society and its organization, as well as of the state and its institutions, in the replacing of a local and territorial economic policy by that of the national state.

—— GUSTAV SCHMOLLER

The end in view was Power: this was furthered by attention to Treasure, Shipping and Population; while these objects could only be obtained by the careful regulation of Industry and Tillage. Such in brief is the *rationale* of the so-called Mercantile System.

—— WILLIAM CUNNINGHAM

Mercantilism is an instrumental concept which . . . should enable us to understand a particular historical period more clearly than we otherwise might.

—— ELI HECKSCHER

As a critical category in terms of which earlier English writers on economics can be appraised "mercantilism" is no longer a particularly useful word. (1937)

—— E. A. J. JOHNSON

Mercantilism had six aspects, not five: the sixth was public (or royal) finance, and one might with great cogency maintain that it was the most important of the lot.

—— HERBERT HEATON

The truth seems to be that there was never a living doctrine at all, nothing that could be compared with vital philosophies of action like physiocracy or liberalism or Marxism. Mercantilism never had a creed; nor was there a priesthood dedicated to its service.

—— ARTHUR V. JUDGES

English mercantilism in its colonial aspects . . . had as its purpose exploitation and, as its means, regulation.

—— LAWRENCE A. HARPER

Mercantilism was not a logical system. It may even be plausibly argued that . . . the much-vaunted mercantile system was not a system at all.

—— RAYMOND DE ROOVER

Mercantilism was a programme, a cause, an adventure. Its aim was the enrichment of the people and its theory looked on this as a work to be done by the creative energy of men organized in a common body.

—— SIR GEORGE CLARK

As a description of a trend of economic thought, the term may well be useful, and worth retaining. As a label for economic policy, it is not simply misleading but actively confusing, a red-herring of historiography. It serves to give a false unity to disparate events, to conceal the close-up reality of particular times and particular circumstances, to blot out the vital intermixture of ideas and preconceptions, of interests and inflences, political and economic, and of the personalities of men, which it is the historian's job to examine.

—— DONALD C. COLEMAN

The obstinate core of mercantilist thought can . . . be seen in the belief that some activities were beneficial and some harmful to the community and that it was the State's task to discern and separate the two.

—— CHARLES WILSON

I. MERCANTILISM—THEORY AND PRACTICE

A Mercantilist Statute

The Statute of Artificers is now regarded as the crowning achievement of the hectic session of parliamentary economic legislation in 1563. The act sought to direct labour into occupations by a system of priorities. First came agriculture, then the crafts ancillary to agriculture, then cloth-making and finally the "higher" trades and professions. To reinforce direction there were regulations designed to stabilize employment and check the mobility of labor. Apprenticeship for seven years was to become universal and compulsory, and no employee was to be engaged for less than a prescribed term, usually a year. The second part of the statute deals with wages, which were to be regulated on an annual basis by the local unpaid magistrates, the justices of the peace (clause XI). For Heckscher this act was "the most ambitious attempt in the whole history of mercantilism to define in a single law a national economic policy." Though abbreviated here, this is still a long and detailed statute which well illustrates the character of economic legislation of the time.

An Act Touching Divers Orders for Artificers, Labourers, Servants of Husbandry and Apprentices [5 *Eliz. c. iv.*] 1563.

I. ALTHOUGH there remain in force presently a great number of statutes concerning . . . apprentices, servants and labourers, as well in husbandry as in divers other . . . occupations, yet partly for the imperfection and contrariety . . . in sundry of the said laws, and for the variety and number of them, and chiefly for that the wages and allowances limited in many of the said statutes are in divers places too small . . . respecting the advancement of prices . . . the said laws cannot conveniently without the greatest grief and burden of the poor labourer and hired man be put in due execution; and as the said statutes were at the time of the making of them thought to be very good and beneficial . . . , as divers of them yet are, so if the substance of as many of the said laws as are meet to be continued shall be digested and reduced into one sole law, and in the same an uniform order prescribed . . . , there is good hope that it will come to pass that the same law, being duly executed, should banish idleness, advance husbandry and yield unto the hired person both in the time of scarcity and in the time of plenty a convenient proportion of wages: Be it therefore enacted. . . . That as much of the statutes heretofore made as concern the hiring, keeping, departing, working, wages or order of servants, workmen, artificers, apprentices and labourers . . . shall be from and after the last day of September next ensuing repealed. . . .

II. No person after the aforesaid last day of September . . . shall be retained, hired or taken into service to work for any less time than for one whole year in any of the sciences . . . or arts of clothiers, woollen

The text of this act is taken from the *Statutes of the Realm*, IV, Part I, 414–22. The spelling has been modernized and the capitalization is in conformity with current practice.

cloth weavers, tuckers, fullers, cloth workers, shearmen, dyers, hosiers, tailors, shoemakers, tanners, pewterers, bakers, brewers, glovers, cutlers, smiths, farriers, curriers, sadlers, spurriers, turners, cappers, hatmakers or feltmakers, bowyers, fletchers, arrowheadmakers, butchers, cooks, or millers.

III. Every person being unmarried and every other person being under the age of thirty years that after the feast of Easter next shall marry, and having been brought up in any of the said arts [etc.] or that hath exercised any of them by the space of three years or more, and not having lands, tenements [etc.] copyhold or freehold of an estate of inheritance or for term of lives of the clear yearly value of 40s. nor being worth of his own goods the clear value of 10l. . . . , not being retained with any person in husbandry or in any of the aforesaid arts . . . nor in any other art, nor in household or in any office with any nobleman, gentleman or others . . . , nor having a convenient farm or other holding in tillage whereupon he may employ his labour, shall (during the time that he shall so be unmarried or under the age of 30 years), upon request made by any person using the art or mystery wherein the said person so required hath been exercised as is aforesaid, be retained and shall not refuse to serve according to the tenor of this Statute upon the pain and penalty hereafter mentioned.

IV. No person which shall retain any servant shall put away his said servant, and no person retained according to this Statute shall depart from his master, mistress or dame before the end of his term, upon the pain hereafter mentioned, unless it be for some reasonable cause to be allowed before two Justices of Peace, or one at the least, or before the mayor or other chief officer of the city, borough or town corporate wherein the said master [etc.] inhabiteth, to whom any of the parties grieved shall complain; which said justices or chief officer shall have the hearing and ordering of the matter between the said master [etc.] and servant, according to the equity of the cause; and

no such master [etc.] shall put away any such servant at the end of his term, or any such servant depart from his said master [etc.] at the end of his term, without one quarter warning given . . . upon the pain hereafter ensuing.

V. Every person between the age of 12 years and the age of 60 years not being lawfully retained nor apprentice with any fisherman or mariner haunting the seas, nor being in service with any carrier of any corn, grain or meal for provision of the city of London, nor with any husbandman in husbandry, nor in any city [etc.] in any of the arts . . . appointed by this Statute to have apprentices, nor being retained . . . for the digging . . . melting . . . making of any silver [or other metals, coal, etc.], nor being occupied in the making of any glass, nor being a gentleman born, nor being a student or scholar in any of the universities or in any school, nor having [lands or goods, as above, section 3], nor having a father or mother then living or other ancestor whose heir apparent he is then having lands [etc.] of the yearly value of £10 or above, or goods or chattels of the value of 40 l., nor being a necessary or convenient officer or servant lawfully retained as is aforesaid, nor having a convenient farm or holding . . . nor being otherwise lawfully retained according to the true meaning of this Statute, shall . . . by virtue of this Statute be compelled to be retained to serve in husbandry by the year with any person that keepth husbandry and will require any such person so to serve.

VI. [Penalty on masters unduly dismissing servants, 40s.: on servants unduly departing or refusing to serve, imprisonment.]

VII. None of the said retained persons in husbandry or in any of the arts or sciences above remembered, after the time of his retainer expired, shall depart forth of one city, town or parish to another nor out of the . . . hundred nor out of the county where he last served, to serve in any other city . . . or county, unless he have a testimonial under the seal of the said city or of the constable or other head officer and of two other honest householders of the city, town or parish where he last served, declaring his lawful departure . . . , which testimonial shall be delivered unto the said servant and also registered by the parson of the parish where such master [etc.] shall dwell. . . .

VIII. [Penalty on a servant departing without such testimonial, imprisonment or whipping; on any one hiring him, 5*l*.]

IX. All artificers and labourers being hired for wages by the day or week shall betwixt the midst of the months of March and September be at their work at or before 5 of the clock in the morning, and continue at work until betwixt 7 and 8 of the clock at night, except it be in the time of breakfast, dinner or drinking, the which times at the most shall not exceed above 2½ hours in the day . . . and all the said artificers and labourers between the midst of September and the midst of March shall be at their work from the spring of the day in the morning until the night of the same day, except it be in time afore appointed for breakfast and dinner, upon pain to forfeit one penny for every hour's absence to be deducted out of his wages.

X. [Penalty on artificers, etc., breaking contract with employers, imprisonment and fine of 5*l*.]

XI. And for the declaration what wages servants, labourers and artificers, either by the year or day or otherwise, shall receive, be it enacted, That the justices of the peace of every shire . . . within the limits of their several commissions . . . and the sheriff of that county if he conveniently may, and every mayor, bailiff or other head officer within any city . . . wherein is any justice of peace, within the limits of the said city . . . shall before the 10th day of June next coming, and afterward yearly at every general sessions first to be holden after Easter, or at some time convenient within six weeks next following Easter, calling unto them such discreet and grave persons of the said county or city as they shall think meet, and conferring together respecting the plenty or scarcity of the time and other cir-

cumstances necessary to be considered, have authority within the limits of their several commissions to rate and appoint the wages as well of such of the said artificers . . . or any other labourer, servant or workman whose wages in time past hath been by any law rated and appointed, as also the wages of all other labourers, artificers [etc.] which have not been rated, as they shall think meet to be rated [etc.] by the year or by the day, week, month or other wise, with meat and drink or without meat and drink, and what wages every workman or labourer shall take by the great for mowing, reaping or threshing [and other agricultural employment] and for any other kind of reasonable labours or service, and shall yearly, before the 12th day of July next after the said assessment made, certify the same . . . with the considerations and causes thereof into the Court of Chancery[1]; whereupon it shall be lawful to the Lord Chancellor of England [or] Lord Keeper upon declaration thereof to the Queen's Majesty . . . or to the Lords and others of the Privy Council to cause to be printed and sent down before the 1st day of September next after the said certificate into every county . . . proclamations containing the several rates appointed . . . with commandment . . . to all persons . . . straitly to observe the same, and to all Justices [etc.] to see the same duly and severely observed . . . ; upon receipt whereof the said Sheriffs, Justices [etc.] shall cause the same proclamation to be entered of record . . . and shall forthwith in open markets upon the market days before Michaelmas then ensuing cause the same proclamation to be proclaimed . . . and to be fixed in some convenient place . . . : and if the said sheriffs, justices [etc.] shall at their said general sessions or at any time after within six weeks . . . think it convenient to retain for the year then to come the rates of wages that they certified the year before or to change them, then they shall before the said 12th day of July yearly certify into the said Court of Chancery their

---

[1] This provision was repealed in 1597.

resolutions, to the intent that proclamations may accordingly be renewed and sent down, and if it shall happen that there be no need of any alteration . . . then the proclamations for the year past shall remain in force. . . .

XII. [Penalty on Justices absent from sessions for rating wages, 5*l*.]

XIII. [Penalty for giving wages higher than the rate, ten days' imprisonment and fine of 5*l*.; for receiving the same, twenty-one days' imprisonment.]

XIV. [Penalty on servants, etc., assaulting masters, etc., one year's imprisonment.]

XV. Provided that in the time of hay or corn harvest the Justices of Peace and also the constable or other head officer of every township upon request . . . may cause all such artificers and persons as be meet to labour . . . to serve by the day for the mowing . . . or inning of corn, grain and hay, and that none of the said persons shall refuse so to do, upon pain to suffer imprisonment in the stocks by the space of two days and one night. . . .

XVI. [Proviso for persons going harvesting into other counties.]

XVII. Two justices of peace, the mayor or other head officer of any city [etc.] and two aldermen or two other discreet burgesses . . . if there be no aldermen, may appoint any such woman as is of the age of 12 years and under the age of 40 years and unmarried and forth of service . . . to be retained or serve by the year or by the week or day for such wages and in such reasonable sort as they shall think meet; and if any such woman shall refuse so to serve, then it shall be lawful for the said justices [etc.] to commit such woman to ward until she shall be bounden to serve as aforesaid.

XVIII. And for the better advancement of husbandry and tillage and to the intent that such as are fit to be made apprentices to husbandry may be bounden thereunto, . . . every person being a householder and having half a ploughland at the least in tillage may receive as an apprentice any person above the age of 10 years and under the age of 18 years to serve in husbandry

until his age of 21 years at the least, or until the age of 24 years as the parties can agree. . . .

XIX. Every person being an householder and 24 years old at the least, dwelling in any city or town corporate and exercising any art, mistery or manual occupation there, may after the feast of St. John Baptist next coming . . . retain the son of any freeman not occupying husbandry nor being a labourer and inhabiting in the same or in any other city or town incorporate, to be bound as an apprentice after the custom and order of the city of London for 7 years at the least, so as the term of such apprentice do not expire afore such apprentice shall be of the age of 24 years at the least.

XX. Provided that it shall not be lawful to any person dwelling in any city or town corporate exercising any of the misteries or crafts of a merchant trafficking into any parts beyond the sea, mercer, draper, goldsmith, ironmonger, embroiderer or clothier that doth put cloth to making and sale, to take any apprentice or servant to be instructed in any of the arts [etc.] which they exercise, except such servant or apprentice be his son, or else that the father or mother of such apprentice or servant shall have . . . lands, tenements [etc.] of the clear yearly value of 40*s*. of one estate of inheritance or freehold at the least. . . .

XXI. From and after the said feast of St. John the Baptist next, it shall be lawful to every person being an householder and 24 years old at the least and not occupying husbandry nor being a labourer dwelling in any town not being incorporate that is a market town . . . and exercising any art, mistery or manual occupation . . . to have in like manner to apprentices the children of any other artificer not occupying husbandry nor being a labourer, which shall inhabit in the same or in any other such market town within the same shire, to serve as apprentices as is aforesaid to any such art [etc.] as hath been usually exercised in any such market town where such apprentice shall be bound.

XXII. Provided that it shall not be lawful to any person dwelling in any such market town exercising the art of a merchant trafficking into the parts beyond the seas, mercer [etc. as above, section XX] to take any apprentice or in any wise to instruct any person in the arts [etc.] last before recited, after the feast of St. John Baptist aforesaid, except such servant or apprentice shall be his son, or else that the father or mother of such apprentice shall have lands [etc.] of the clear yearly value of 3*l*. of one estate of inheritance or freehold at the least. . . .

XXIII. From and after the said feast it shall be lawful to any person exercising the art of a smith, wheelwright, ploughwright, millwright, carpenter, rough mason, plaisterer, sawyer, lime-burner, brickmaker, bricklayer, tiler, slater, healyer, tilemaker, linen-weaver, turner, cooper, millers, earthen potters, woollen weaver weaving housewives' or household cloth only and none other, cloth-fuller otherwise called tucker or walker, burner of ore and wood ashes, thatcher or shingler, wheresoever he shall dwell, to have the son of any person as apprentice . . . albeit the father or mother of any such apprentice have not any lands, tenements or hereditaments.

XXIV. After the first day of May next coming it shall not be lawful to any person, other than such as now do lawfully exercise any art, mistery or manual occupation, to exercise any craft now used within the realm of England or Wales, except he shall have been brought up therein seven years at the least as apprentice in manner abovesaid, nor to set any person on work in such occupation being not a workman at this day, except he shall have been apprentice as is aforesaid, or else having served as an apprentice will become a journeyman or be hired by the year; upon pain that every person willingly offending shall forfeit for every default 40*s*. for every month.

XXV. Provided that no person exercising the art of a woollen cloth weaver, other than such as be inhabiting within the counties of Cumberland, Westmoreland, Lancaster, and Wales, weaving friezes, cottons or housewives' cloth only, making and weaving woollen cloth commonly sold by any clothier, shall have any apprentice or shall instruct any person in the science of weaving aforesaid in any place (cities, towns corporate, and market towns only except), unless such person be his son, or else that the father or mother of such apprentice or servant shall . . . have lands [etc.] to the clear yearly value of 3*l*. of an estate of inheritance or freehold . . . upon pain of forfeiture of 20*s*. for every month.

XXVI. Every person that shall have three apprentices in any of the said crafts of a cloth-maker, fuller, shearman, weaver, tailor or shoemaker shall keep one journeyman, and for every other apprentice above the number of the said three apprentices one other journeyman, upon pain of every default therein, 10*l*.

XXVII. [Proviso for worsted-makers of Norwich.]

XXVIII. If any person shall be required by any householder having half a ploughland at the least in tillage to be an apprentice and to serve in husbandry, or in any other kind of art before expressed, and shall refuse so to do, then upon the complaint of such housekeeper made to one Justice of Peace of the county wherein the said refusal is made, or of such householder inhabiting in any city, town corporate, or market town to the mayor, bailiffs or head officer of the said city [etc.] . . . they shall have full power to send for the same person so refusing; and if the said Justice or head officer shall think the said person meet to serve as an apprentice in that art . . . the said Justice or head officer shall have power . . . to commit him unto ward, there to remain until he will be bounden to serve . . . and if any such master shall evil entreat his apprentice . . . or the apprentice do not his duty to his master, then the said master or apprentice being grieved shall repair unto one Justice of Peace within the said county or to the head officer of the place where the said master dwelleth, who shall . . . take such order and direction between the said master and his apprentice as the equity of the case shall require; and if for want of good conformity in the said master the said Justice or head officer cannot compound the matter between him and his apprentice, then the said Justice or head officer shall take bond of the said master to appear at the next sessions then to be holden in the said county or within the said city [etc.] . . . and upon his appearance and hearing of the matter . . . if it be thought meet unto them to discharge the said apprentice, then the said Justices or four of them at the least, whereof one to be of the quorum, or the said head officer, with the consent of three other of his brethren or men of best reputation within the said city [etc.] shall have power . . . to pronounce that they have discharged the said apprentice of his apprenticehood . . . : and if the default shall be found to be in the apprentice, then the said Justices or head officer, with the assistants aforesaid, shall cause such due punishment to be ministered unto him as by their wisdom and discretions shall be thought meet.

XXIX. Provided that no person shall by force of this Statute be bounden to enter into any apprenticeship, other than such as be under the age of 21 years.

XXX. And to the end that this Statute may from time to time be . . . put in good execution . . . be it enacted, That the Jus-tices of Peace of every county, dividing themselves into several limits, and likewise every mayor or head officer of any city or town corporate, shall yearly between the feast of St. Michael the Archangel and the Nativity of our Lord, and between the feast of the Annunciation of our Lady and the feast of the Nativity of St. John Baptist . . . make a special and diligent inquiry of the branches and articles of this Statute and of the good execution of the same, and where they shall find any defaults to see the same severely corrected and punished without favour . . . or displeasure.

XXXI. . . . Every Justice of Peace, mayor, or head officer, for every day that he shall sit in the execution of this Statute, shall have allowed unto him 5s. to be paid . . . of the fines [etc.] due by force of this Statute. . . .

XXXII. [Procedure for recovery of penalties.]

XXXIII. Provided always that this Act shall not be prejudicial to the cities of London and Norwich, or to the lawful liberties [etc.] of the same cities for the having of apprentices.

XXXIV. [Contracts of apprenticeship contrary to this Act to be void, and a penalty of 10l.]

XXXV. [Contracts of apprenticeship to hold good though made while the apprentice is under age.]

The Balance of Trade Argument

THOMAS MUN

Thomas Mun (1571–1641) was the son of a London mercer. As a youth he engaged in trade, particularly with Italy and the Levant, and later, in 1615, he became a director of the East India Company, a position he held until his death. In 1621 he published a defense of the company's activities, *A Discourse of Trade from England unto the East Indies*, and a few years later wrote *England's Treasure by Foreign Trade*, which was published posthumously in 1664. In the passages printed below,—Chapters 2 and 4—the balance of trade argument is set out.

II. THE MEANS TO ENRICH THIS KINGDOM, AND TO INCREASE OUR TREASURE

Although a kingdom may be enriched by gifts received, or by purchase taken from some other nations, yet these are things uncertain and of small consideration when they happen. The ordinary means therefore to increase our wealth and treasure is by foreign trade, wherein we must ever observe this rule; to sell more to strangers yearly than we consume of theirs in value. For suppose that when this kingdom is plentifully served with the cloth, lead, tin, iron, fish and other native commodities, we do yearly export the surplus to foreign countries to the value of twenty-two hundred thousand pounds; by which means we are enabled beyond the seas to buy and bring in foreign wares for our use and consumptions, to the value of twenty hundred thousand pounds; by this order duly kept in our trading, we may rest assured that the kingdom shall be enriched yearly two hundred thousand pounds, which must be brought to us in so much treasure; because that part of our stock which is not returned to us in wares must necessarily be brought home in treasure.

For in this case it comes to pass in the stock of a kingdom, as in the estate of a private man; who is supposed to have one thousand pounds yearly revenue and two thousand pounds of ready money in his chest: if such a man through excess shall spend one thousand five hundred pounds per annum, all his ready money will be gone in four years; and in the like time his said money will be doubled if he take a frugal course to spend but five hundred pounds per annum; which rule never fails likewise in the commonwealth, but in some cases (of no great moment) which I will hereafter declare, when I shall shew by whom and in what manner this balance of the kingdom's account ought to be drawn up yearly, or so often as it shall please the state to discover how much we gain or lose by trade with foreign nations. But first I will say something concerning those ways and means which will increase our exportations and diminish our importations of wares; which being done, I will then set down some other arguments both affirmative and negative to strengthen that which is here declared, and thereby to shew that all the other means which are commonly supposed to enrich the kingdom with treasure are altogether insufficient and mere fallacies.

*   *   *

From Thomas Mun, *England's Treasure by Foreign Trade* (Reprint of the first edition of 1664, Oxford, 1928), 5–6, 14–19.

IV. THE EXPORTATION OF OUR MONEY IN TRADE OF MERCHANDIZE IS A MEANS TO INCREASE OUR TREASURE

This position is so contrary to the common opinion that it will require many and strong arguments to prove it before it can be accepted by the multitude, who bitterly exclaim when they see any money carried out of the realm; affirming thereupon that we have absolutely lost so much treasure, and that this is an act directly against the long continued laws made and confirmed by the wisdom of this kingdom in the High Court of Parliament, and that many places, nay Spain itself which is the fountain of money, forbids the exportation thereof, some cases only excepted. To all which I might answer, that Venice, Florence, Genoa, the Low Countries and divers other places permit it, their people applaud it, and find great benefit by it; but all this makes a noise and proves nothing and we must therefore come to those reasons which concern the business in question.

We have already supposed our yearly consumptions of foreign wares to be for the value of twenty hundred thousand pounds, and our exportations to exceed that two hundred thousand pounds, which sum we have thereupon affirmed is brought to us in treasure to balance the account. But now if we add three hundred thousand pounds more in ready money unto our former exportations in wares, what profit can we have (will some men say) although by this means we should bring in so much ready money more than we did before, seeing that we have carried out the like value.

To this the answer is, that when we have prepared our exportations of wares, and sent out as much of everything as we can spare or vent [sell] abroad, it is not therefore said that then we should add our money thereunto to fetch in more money immediately, but rather first to enlarge our trade by enabling us to bring in more foreign wares, which being sent out again will in due time much increase our treasure.

For although in this manner we yearly multiply our importations to the mainte-nance of more shipping and mariners, improvement of His Majesty's Customs and other benefits, yet our consumption of those foreign wares is no more than it was before; so that all the said increase of commodities brought in by the means of our ready money sent out as described above, in the end becomes an exportation of far greater value to us than our said money was, which is proved by three examples, as follows:

1. For I suppose that £100,000 being sent in our shipping to East Countries [the Baltic] will buy there one hundred thousand quarters of wheat clear aboard the ships, which after being brought into England and housed, to export the same at the best time for vent thereof in Spain or Italy, it cannot yield less in those parts than two hundred thousand pounds to make the merchant but a saver, yet by this reckoning we see the kingdom hath doubled that treasure.

2. Again this profit will be far greater when we trade thus in remote countries, as, for example, if we send one hundred thousand pounds into the East Indies to buy pepper there, and bring it hither, and from hence send it for Italy or Turkey, it must yield seven hundred thousand pounds at least in those places, in regard of the excessive charge which the merchant disburses in those long voyages in shipping, wages, victuals, insurance, interest, customs, imposts, and the like, all which notwithstanding the king and the kingdom gets.

3. But where the voyages are short and the wares rich, which therefore will not employ much shipping, the profit will be far less. As when another hundred thousand pounds shall be employed in Turkey in raw silks, and brought hither to be transported after from hence into France, the Low Countries, or Germany, the merchant shall have good gain, although he sell it there but for one hundred and fifty thousand pounds: and thus take the voyages al-

together in their medium, the money exported will be returned to us more than trebled. But if any man will yet object, that these returns come to us in wares, and not really in money as they were issued out, the answer is (keeping our first ground) that if our consumption of foreign wares be no more yearly than is already supposed, and our exportations be so mightily increased by this manner of trading with ready money as is before declared, it is not then possible but that all the overbalance or difference should return either in money or in such wares as we must export again, which, as is already plainly shewn, will be still a greater means to increase our treasure.

For it is in the stock of the kingdom as in the estates of private men, who having a store of wares, do not therefore say that they will not venture out or trade with their money (for this were ridiculous) but do also turn that into wares, whereby they multiply their money, and so by a continual and orderly change of one into the other grow rich, and when they please turn all their estates into treasure; for they that have wares cannot want money.

Neither is it said that money is the life of trade, as if it could not subsist without the same; for we know that there was great trading by way of commutation or barter when there was little money stirring in the world. The Italians and some other nations have such remedies against this want, that it can neither decay nor hinder their trade, for they transfer bills of debt, and have banks both public and private, wherein they do assign their credits from one to another daily for very great sums with ease and satisfaction by writings only, whilst in the meantime the mass of treasure which gave foundation to these credits is employed in foreign trade as a merchandize, and by the said means they have little other use of money in those countries more than for their ordinary expenses. It is not therefore the keeping of our money in the kingdom, but the necessity and use of our wares in foreign countries, and our want of their commodities that causes the vent and consumption on all sides, which makes a quick and ample trade. If we were once poor, and now having gained some store of money by trade with resolution to keep it still in the realm, shall this cause other nations to spend more of our commodities than formerly they have done, whereby we might say that our trade is quickened and enlarged? No verily, it will produce no such good effect: but rather according to the alteration of times by their true causes we may expect the contrary; for all men do consent that plenty of money in a kingdom makes the native commodities dearer, which as it is to the profit of some private men in their revenues, so is it directly against the benefit of the public in the quantity of the trade; for as plenty of money makes wares dearer, so dear wares decline their use and consumption. And although this is a very hard lesson for some great landed men to learn, yet I am sure it is a true lesson for all the land to observe, lest when we have gained some store of money by trade we lose it again by not trading with our money. I knew a Prince in Italy (of famous memory) Ferdinando the first, great Duke of Tuscany, who being very rich in treasure, endeavoured therewith to enlarge his trade by issuing out to his merchants great sums of money for very small profit; I myself had forty thousand crowns of him gratis for a whole year, although he knew that I would presently send it away in specie for the parts of Turkey to be employed in wares for his countries, he being well assured that in this course of trade it would return again (according to the old saying) with a duck in the mouth. This noble and industrious prince by his care and diligence to countenance and favour merchants in their affairs, did so increase the practice thereof, that there is scarcely a nobleman or gentleman in all his dominions that does not merchandize either by himself or in partnership with others, whereby within these thirty years the trade to his port of Leghorn is so much increased, that of a poor little town (as I myself knew it) it is now become a fair and strong city, being one of the most famous places for trade in all Christendom. And yet it is worthy of our observation that the multitude of ships and wares which come from England, the Low Countries, and other places, have little or no means to make their returns from thence but only in ready money, which they may and do carry away freely at all times, to the incredible advantage of the said great Duke of Tuscany and his subjects, who are much enriched by the continual great concourse of merchants from all the states of the neighbour princes, bringing them plenty of money daily to supply their wants of the said wares. And thus we see that the current of merchandize which carries away their treasure becomes a flowing stream to fill them again in a greater measure with money.

There is yet an objection or two as weak as all the rest: that is, if we trade with our money we shall issue out the less wares; as if a man should say, those countries which previously had occasion to consume our cloth, lead, tin, iron, fish, and the like, shall now make use of our money in the place of those necessities, which were most absurd to affirm, or that the merchant had not rather carry out wares by which there is ever some gains expected, than to export money which is still but the same without any increase.

But on the contrary there are many countries which may yield us very profitable trade for our money, which otherwise afford us no trade at all because they have no use of our wares, as namely the East Indies for one in the first beginning thereof, although since by industry in our commerce with those nations we have brought them into the use of much of our lead, cloth, tin, and other things, which is a good addition to the former vent of our commodities.

Again, some men have alleged that those countries which permit money to be carried out, do it because they have few or no wares to trade withall: but we have great store of commodities, and therefore their action ought not to be our example.

To this the answer is briefly that if we have such a quantity of wares as fully provide us with all things needed from beyond the seas, why should we then doubt that our money sent out in trade must not necessarily come back again in treasure together with the great gains which it may procure in such manner as is before set down? And on the other side, if those nations which send out their monies do it because they have but few wares of their own, how come they then have so much treasure as we ever see in those places which suffer it freely to be exported at all times and by whomsoever? I answer, Even by trading with their money; for by what other means can they get it, having no mines of gold or silver?

Thus may we plainly see that when this weighty business is duly considered in his end, as all our humane actions ought well to be weighed, it is found much contrary to that which most men esteem thereof, because they search no further than the beginning of the work, which misinforms their judgments, and leads them into error. For if we only behold the actions of the husbandman in the seed-time when he casts away much good corn into the ground, we will rather account him a mad man than a husbandman: but when we consider his labours in the harvest which is the end of his endeavours, we find the worth and plentiful increase of his actions.

II. ADAM SMITH AND NINETEENTH-CENTURY VIEWS

The Classical Critic

ADAM SMITH

Adam Smith (1723–90) was born the son of the comptroller of customs at Kirkaldy, Scotland. For a time professor of moral philosophy at the University of Glasgow, he wrote *The Wealth of Nations* while employed as traveling tutor to the Duke of Buccleuch. Its publication in 1766 was a major landmark in the history of economics. Two years later Smith became commissioner of customs at Edinburgh, a post he held till his death. The passages which follow taken from Book IV, entitled "Of the Principle of the Commercial or Mercantile System," sets out Adam Smith's criticism of what he regarded as the basic mercantile fallacies: the confusion of wealth with gold and a favorable balance of trade with the annual balance of income over consumption. Further, the mercantile system, he argues, was designed to benefit a section of the community (merchants and manufacturers) rather than the nation as a whole.

THE DIFFERENT progress of opulence in different ages and nations, has given occasion to two different systems of political oeconomy, with regard to enriching the people. The one may be called the system of commerce, the other that of agriculture. I shall endeavour to explain both as fully and distinctly as I can, and shall begin with the system of commerce. It is the modern system, and is best understood in our own country and in our own times.

*　　*　　*

That wealth consists in money, or in gold and silver, is a popular notion which naturally arises from the double function of money, as the instrument of commerce, and as the measure of value. In consequence of its being the instrument of commerce, when we have money we can more readily obtain whatever else we have occasion for, than by means of any other commodity. The great affair, we always find, is to get money. When that is obtained, there is no difficulty in making any subsequent purchase. In consequence of its being the measure of value, we estimate that of all other commodities by the quantity of money which they will exchange for. We say of a rich man that he is worth a great deal, and of a poor man that he is worth very little money. A frugal man, or a man eager to be rich, is said to love money; and a careless, a generous, or a profuse man, is said to be indifferent about it. To grow rich is to get money; and wealth and money, in short, are, in common language, considered as in every respect synonymous.

. . . If a nation could be separated from all the world, it would be of no conse-

From Adam Smith, *An Inquiry into the Nature and Causes of the Wealth of Nations* (Cannan edition, Methuen, 1904), I, 396–417.

quence how much, or how little money circulated in it. The consumable goods which were circulated by means of this money, would only be exchanged for a greater or a smaller number of pieces; but the real wealth or poverty of the country, they allow, would depend altogether upon the abundance or scarcity of those consumable goods. But it is otherwise, they think, with countries which have connections with foreign nations, and which are obliged to carry on foreign wars, and to maintain fleets and armies in distant countries. This, they say, cannot be done, but by sending abroad money to pay them with; and a nation cannot send much money abroad, unless it has a good deal at home. Every such nation, therefore, must endeavour in time of peace to accumulate gold and silver, that, when occasion requires, it may have wherewithal to carry on foreign wars.

In consequence of these popular notions, all the different nations of Europe have studied, though to little purpose, every possible means of accumulating gold and silver in their respective countries. Spain and Portugal, the proprietors of the principal mines which supply Europe with those metals, have either prohibited their exportation under the severest penalties, or subjected it to a considerable duty. The like prohibition seems anciently to have made a part of the policy of most other European nations. It is even to be found, where we should least of all expect to find it, in some old Scotch acts of parliament, which forbid under heavy penalties the carrying gold or silver *forth of the kingdom*. The like policy anciently took place both in France and England.

When those countries became commercial, the merchants found this prohibition, upon many occasions, extremely inconvenient. They could frequently buy more advantageously with gold and silver than with any other commodity, the foreign goods which they wanted, either to import into their own, or to carry to some other foreign country. They remonstrated, therefore, against this prohibition as hurtful to trade.

They represented, first, that the exportation of gold and silver in order to purchase foreign goods, did not always diminish the quantity of those metals in the kingdom. That, on the contrary, it might frequently increase that quantity; because, if the consumption of foreign goods was not thereby increased in the country, those goods might be re-exported to foreign countries, and, being there sold for a large profit, might bring back much more treasure than was originally sent out to purchase them. Mr. Mun compares this operation of foreign trade to the seed-time and harvest of agriculture. "If we only behold," says he, "the actions of the husbandman in the seed-time, when he casteth away much good corn into the ground, we shall account him rather a madman than a husbandman. But when we consider his labours in the harvest, which is the end of his endeavours, we shall find the worth and plentiful increase of his actions."

They represented, secondly, that this prohibition could not hinder the exportation of gold and silver, which, on account of the smallness of their bulk in proportion to their value, could easily be smuggled abroad. That this exportation could only be prevented by a proper attention to, what they called, the balance of trade. That when the country exported to a greater value than it imported, a balance became due to it from foreign nations, which was necessarily paid to it in gold and silver, and thereby increased the quantity of those metals in the kingdom. But that when it imported to a greater value than it exported, a contrary balance became due to foreign nations, which was necessarily paid to them in the same manner, and thereby diminished that quantity. That in this case to prohibit the exportation of those metals could not prevent it, but only by making it more dangerous, render it more expensive. That the exchange was thereby turned more against the country which owed the balance, than it otherwise might have been; the merchant who purchased a bill upon the foreign country being obliged to pay the banker who sold it, not only for the natural risk, trouble and expence of sending the money thither, but for the extraordinary risk arising from the prohibition. But that the more the exchange was against any country, the more the balance of trade became necessarily against it; the money of that country becoming necessarily of so much less value, in comparison with that of the country to which the balance was due. That if the exchange between England and Holland, for example, was five per cent against England, it would require a hundred and five ounces of silver in England to purchase a bill for a hundred ounces of silver in Holland: that a hundred and five ounces of silver in England, therefore, would be worth only a hundred ounces of silver in Holland, and would purchase only a proportionable quantity of Dutch goods: but that a hundred ounces of silver in Holland, on the contrary, would be worth a hundred and five ounces in England, and would purchase a proportionable quantity of English goods: that the English goods which were sold to Holland would be sold so much cheaper; and the Dutch goods which were sold to England, so much dearer, by the difference of the exchange; that the one would draw so much less Dutch money to England, and the other so much more English money to Holland, as this difference amounted to: and that the balance of trade, therefore, would necessarily be so much more against England, and would require a greater balance of gold and silver to be exported to Holland.

Those arguments were partly solid and partly sophistical. They were solid so far as they asserted that the exportation of gold and silver in trade might frequently be advantageous to the country. They were solid too, in asserting that no prohibition could prevent their exportation, when private people found any advantage in exporting them. But they were sophistical in supposing, that either to preserve or to augment the quantity of those metals required more the attention of government, than to preserve or to augment the quantity of any

other useful commodities, which the freedom of trade, without any such attention, never fails to supply in the proper quantity. They were sophistical too, perhaps, in asserting that the high price of exchange necessarily increased, what they called, the unfavourable balance of trade, or occasioned the exportation of a greater quantity of gold and silver. That high price, indeed, was extremely disadvantageous to the merchants who had any money to pay in foreign countries. They paid so much dearer for the bills which their bankers granted them upon those countries. But though the risk arising from the prohibition might occasion some extraordinary expence to the bankers, it would not necessarily carry any more money out of the country. This expence would generally be all laid out in the country, in smuggling the money out of it, and could seldom occasion the exportation of a single six-pence beyond the precise sum drawn for. The high price of exchange too would naturally dispose the merchants to endeavour to make their exports nearly balance their imports, in order that they might have this high exchange to pay upon as small a sum as possible. The high price of exchange, besides, must necessarily have operated as a tax, in raising the price of foreign goods, and thereby diminishing their consumption. It would tend, therefore, not to increase, but to diminish, what they called, the unfavourable balance of trade, and consequently the exportation of gold and silver.

Such as they were, however, those arguments convinced the people to whom they were addressed. They were addressed by merchants to parliaments, and to the councils of princes, to nobles, and to country gentlemen; by those who were supposed to understand trade, to those who were conscious to themselves that they knew nothing about the matter. That foreign trade enriched the country, experience demonstrated to the nobles and country gentlemen, as well as to the merchants; but how, or in what manner, none of them well knew. The merchants knew perfectly in what manner it enriched themselves. It was their business to know it. But to know in what manner it enriched the country, was no part of their business. This subject never came into their consideration, but when they had occasion to apply to their country for some change in the laws relating to foreign trade. It then became necessary to say something about the beneficial effects of foreign trade, and the manner in which those effects were obstructed by the laws as they then stood. To the judges who were to decide the business, it appeared a most satisfactory account of the matter, when they were told that foreign trade brought money into the country, but that the laws in question hindered it from bringing so much as it otherwise would do. Those arguments therefore produced the wished-for effect. The prohibition of exporting gold and silver was in France and England confined to the coin of those respective countries. The exportation of foreign coin and of bullion was made free. In Holland, and in some other places, this liberty was extended even to the coin of the country. The attention of government was turned away from guarding against the exportation of gold and silver, to watch over the balance of trade, as the only cause which could occasion any augmentation or diminution of those metals. From one fruitless care it was turned away to another care much more intricate, much more embarrassing, and just equally fruitless. The title of Mun's book, England's Treasure in Foreign Trade, became a fundamental maxim in the political oeconomy, not of England only, but of all other commercial countries. The inland or home trade, the most important of all, the trade in which an equal capital affords the greatest revenue, and creates the greatest employment to the people of the country, was considered as subsidiary only to foreign trade. It neither brought money into the country, it was said, nor carried any out of it. The country therefore could never become either richer or poorer by means of it, except so far as its prosperity or decay might

indirectly influence the state of foreign trade. . . .

A country that has no mines of its own must undoubtedly draw its gold and silver from foreign countries, in the same manner as one that has no vineyards of its own must draw its wines. It does not seem necessary, however, that the attention of government should be more turned towards the one than towards the other object. A country that has wherewithal to buy wine, will always get the wine which it has occasion for; and a country that has wherewithal to buy gold and silver, will never be in want of those metals. They are to be bought for a certain price like all other commodities, and as they are the price of all other commodities, so all other commodities are the price of those metals. We trust with perfect security that the freedom of trade, without any attention of government, will always supply us with the wine which we have occasion for: and we may trust with equal security that it will always supply us with all the gold and silver which we can afford to purchase or to employ, either in circulating our commodities, or in other uses.

The quantity of every commodity which human industry can either purchase or produce, naturally regulates itself in every country according to the effectual demand, or according to the demand of those who are willing to pay the whole rent, labour and profits which must be paid in order to prepare and bring it to market. But no commodities regulate themselves more easily or more exactly according to this effectual demand than gold and silver; because, on account of the small bulk and great value of those metals, no commodities can be more easily transported from one place to another, from the places where they are cheap, to those where they are dear, from the places where they exceed, to those where they fall short of this effectual demand. If there were in England, for example, an effectual demand for an additional quantity of gold, a packet-boat could bring from Lisbon, or from wherever else it was to be had, fifty tuns of gold, which could be coined into more than five millions of guineas. But if there were an effectual demand for grain to the same value, to import it would require, at five guineas a tun, a million of tuns of shipping, or a thousand ships of a thousand tuns each. The navy of England would not be sufficient.

When the quantity of gold and silver imported into any country exceeds the effectual demand, no vigilance of government can prevent their exportation. All the sanguinary laws of Spain and Portugal are not able to keep their gold and silver at home. The continual importations from Peru and Brazil exceed the effectual demand of those countries, and sink the price of those metals there below that in the neighbouring countries. If, on the contrary, in any particular country their quantity fell short of the effectual demand, so as to raise their price above that of the neighbouring countries, the government would have no occasion to take any pains to import them. If it were even to take pains to prevent their importation, it would not be able to effectuate it. Those metals, when the Spartans had got wherewithal to purchase them, broke through all the barriers which the laws of Lycurgus opposed to their entrance into Lacedemon. All the sanguinary laws of the customs are not able to prevent the importation of the teas of the Dutch and Gottenburgh East India companies; because somewhat cheaper than those of the British company. A pound of tea, however, is about a hundred times the bulk of one of the highest prices, sixteen shillings, that is commonly paid for it in silver, and more than two thousand times the bulk of the same price in gold, and consequently just so many times more difficult to smuggle.

It is partly owing to the easy transportation of gold and silver from the places where they abound to those where they are wanted, that the price of those metals does not fluctuate continually like that of the greater part of other commodities, which are hindered by their bulk from shifting their situation, when the market happens to be either over or under-stocked with them. The price of those metals, indeed, is not altogether exempted from variation, but the changes to which it is liable are generally slow, gradual, and uniform. In Europe, for example, it is supposed, without much foundation, perhaps, that, during the course of the present and preceding century, they have been constantly, but gradually, sinking in their value, on account of the continual importations from the Spanish West Indies. But to make any sudden change in the price of gold and silver, so as to raise or lower at once, sensibly and remarkably, the money price of all other commodities, requires such a revolution in commerce as that occasioned by the discovery of America.

If, notwithstanding all this, gold and silver should at any time fall short in a country which has wherewithal to purchase them, there are more expedients for supplying their place, than that of almost any other commodity. If the materials of manufacture are wanted, industry must stop. If provisions are wanted, the people must starve. But if money is wanted, barter will supply its place, though with a good deal of inconveniency. Buying and selling upon credit, and the different dealers compensating their credits with one another, once a month or once a year, will supply it with less inconveniency. A well-regulated paper money will supply it, not only without any inconveniency, but, in some cases, with some advantages. Upon every account, therefore, the attention of government never was so unnecessarily employed, as when directed to watch over the preservation or increase of the quantity of money in any country.

No complaint, however, is more common than that of a scarcity of money. Money, like wine, must always be scarce with those who have neither wherewithal to buy it, nor credit to borrow it. Those who have either, will seldom be in want either of the money, or of the wine which they have occasion for. This complaint, however, of the scarcity of money, is not always confined to improvident spendthrifts. It is sometimes general through a whole mercantile town, and the country in its neighbourhood. Over-trading is the common cause of it. Sober men, whose projects have been disproportioned to their capitals, are as likely to have neither wherewithal to buy money, nor credit to borrow it, as prodigals whose expence has been disproportioned to their revenue. Before their projects can be brought to bear, their stock is gone, and their credit with it. They run about everywhere to borrow money, and every body tells them that they have none to lend. Even such general complaints of the scarcity of money do not always prove that the usual number of gold and silver pieces are not circulating in the country, but that many people want those pieces who have nothing to give for them. When the profits of trade happen to be greater than ordinary, over-trading becomes a general error both among great and small dealers. They do not always send more money abroad than usual, but they buy upon credit both at home and abroad, an unusual quantity of goods, which they send to some distant market, in hopes that the returns will come in before the demand for payment. The demand comes before the returns, and they have nothing at hand, with which they can either purchase money, or give solid security for borrowing. It is not any scarcity of gold and silver, but the difficulty which such people find in borrowing, and which their creditors find in getting payment, that occasions the general complaint of the scarcity of money.

It would be too ridiculous to go about seriously to prove, that wealth does not consist in money, or in gold and silver; but in what money purchases, and is valuable only for purchasing. Money, no doubt, makes always a part of the national capital; but it has already been shown that it generally makes but a small part, and always the most unprofitable part of it.

*   *   *

It is not always necessary to accumulate gold and silver, in order to enable a country to carry on foreign wars, and to maintain fleets and armies in distant countries. Fleets and armies are maintained, not with gold and silver, but with consumable goods. The nation which, from the annual produce of its domestic industry, from the annual revenue arising out of its lands, labour, and consumable stock, has wherewithal to purchase those consumable goods in distant countries, can maintain foreign wars there.

A nation may purchase the pay and provisions of an army in a distant country three different ways; by sending abroad either, first, some part of its accumulated gold and silver; or secondly, some part of the annual produce of its manufactures; or last of all, some part of its annual rude produce.

The gold and silver which can properly be considered as accumulated or stored up in any country, may be distinguished into three parts; first, the circulating money; secondly, the plate of private families; and last of all, the money which may have been collected by many years parsimony, and laid up in the treasury of the prince. . . .

It can seldom happen that much can be spared from the circulating money of the country; because in that there can seldom be much redundancy. The value of goods annually bought and sold in any country requires a certain quantity of money to circulate and distribute them to their proper consumers, and can give employment to no more. The channel of circulation necessarily draws to itself a sum sufficient to fill it, and never admits any more. Something, however, is generally withdrawn from this channel in the case of foreign war. By the great number of people who are maintained abroad, fewer are maintained at home. Fewer goods are circulated there, and less money becomes necessary to circulate them. An extraordinary quantity of paper money, of some sort or other too, such as exchequer notes, navy bills, and bank bills in England, is generally issued upon such occasions, and by supplying the place of circulating gold and silver, gives an opportunity of sending a greater quantity of it abroad. All this, however, could afford but a poor resource for maintaining a foreign war, of great expence and several years duration.

The melting down the plate of private families, has upon every occasion been found a still more insignificant one. The French, in the beginning of the last war, did not derive so much advantage from this expedient as to compensate the loss of the fashion.

The accumulated treasures of the prince have, in former times, afforded a much greater and more lasting resource. In the present times, if you except the king of Prussia, to accumulate treasure seems to be no part of the policy of European princes.

The funds which maintained the foreign wars of the present century, the most expensive perhaps which history records, seem to have had little dependency upon the exportation either of the circulating money, or of the plate of private families, or of the treasure of the prince. . . .

The enormous expence of the late war, therefore, must have been chiefly defrayed, not by the exportation of gold and silver, but by that of British commodities of some kind or other. When the government, or those who acted under them, contracted with a merchant for a remittance to some foreign country, he would naturally endeavour to pay his foreign correspondent, upon whom he had granted a bill, by sending abroad rather commodities than gold and silver. If the commodities of Great Britain were not in demand in that country, he would endeavour to send them to some other country, in which he could purchase a bill upon that country. The transportation of commodities, when properly suited to the market, is always attended with a considerable profit; whereas that of gold and silver is scarce ever attended with any. When those metals are sent abroad in order to purchase foreign commodities, the merchant's profit arises, not from the purchase, but from the sale of the returns. But when they are sent abroad merely to pay a debt, he gets no returns, and consequently no profit. He naturally, therefore, exerts his invention to find out a way of paying his foreign debts, rather by the exportation of commodities than by that of gold and silver. The great quantity of British goods exported during the course of the late war, without bringing back any returns, is accordingly remarked by the author of The Present State of the Nation. . . .

The commodities most proper for being transported to distant countries, in order to purchase there, either the pay and provisions of an army, or some part of the money of the mercantile republic to be employed in purchasing them, seem to be the finer and more improved manufactures; such as contain a great value in a small bulk, and can, therefore, be exported to a great distance at little expence. A country whose industry produces a great annual surplus of such manufactures, which are usually exported to foreign countries, may carry on for many years a very expensive foreign war, without either exporting any considerable quantity of gold and silver, or even having any such quantity to export. A considerable part of the annual surplus of its manufactures must, indeed, in this case be exported, without bringing back any returns to the country, though it does to the merchant; the government purchasing of the merchant his bills upon foreign countries, in order to purchase there the pay and provisions of an army. Some part of this surplus, however, may still continue to bring back a return. The manufacturers, during the war, will have a double demand upon them, and be called upon, first, to work up goods to be sent abroad, for paying the bills drawn upon foreign countries for the pay and provisions of the army; and, secondly, to work up such as are necessary for purchasing the common returns that had usually been consumed in the country. In the midst of the most destructive foreign war, therefore, the greater part of manufactures may frequently flourish greatly; and, on the contrary, they may decline on the return of the peace. They may flourish amidst the ruin of their country, and begin to decay upon the return of its prosperity. The different state of many different branches of the British manufactures during the late war, and for some time after the peace, may serve as an illustration of what has been just now said.

No foreign war of great expence or duration could conveniently be carried on by the exportation of the rude produce of the soil. The expence of sending such a quantity of it to a foreign country as might purchase the pay and provisions of an army, would be too great. Few countries too produce much more rude produce than what is sufficient for the subsistence of their own inhabitants. To send abroad any great quantity of it, therefore, would be to send abroad a part of the necessary subsistence of the people. It is otherwise with the exportation of manufactures. The maintenance of the people employed in them is kept at home, and only the surplus part of their work is exported.

* * *

The importation of gold and silver is not the principal, much less the sole benefit which a nation derives from its foreign trade. Between whatever places foreign trade is carried on, they all of them derive two distinct benefits from it. It carries out that surplus part of the produce of their land and labour for which there is no demand among them, and brings back in return for it something else for which there is a demand. It gives a value to their superfluities, by exchanging them for something else, which may satisfy a part of their wants, and increase their enjoyments. By means of it, the narrowness of the home market does not hinder the division of labour in any particular branch of art or manufacture from being carried to the highest perfection. By opening a more extensive market for whatever part of the produce of their labour may exceed the home consumption, it encourages them to improve its productive powers, and to augment its annual produce to the utmost, and thereby to increase the real revenue and wealth of the society. These great and important services foreign trade is continually occupied in performing, to all the different countries between which it is carried on. They all derive great benefit from it, though that in which the merchant resides generally derives the greatest, as he is generally more employed in supplying the wants, and carrying out the superfluities of his own, than of any other particular country. To import the gold and silver which may be wanted, into the countries which have no mines, is, no doubt, a part of the business of foreign commerce. It is, however, a most insignificant part of it. A country which carried on foreign trade merely upon this account, could scarce have occasion to freight a ship in a century.

It is not by the importation of gold and silver, that the discovery of America has enriched Europe. By the abundance of the American mines, those metals have become cheaper. A service of plate can now be purchased for about a third part of the corn, or a third part of the labour, which it would have cost in the fifteenth century. With the same annual expence of labour and commodities, Europe can annually purchase about three times the quantity of plate which it could have purchased at that time. But when a commodity comes to be sold for a third part of what had been its usual price, not only those who purchased it before can purchase three times their former quantity, but it is brought down to the level of a much greater number of purchasers, perhaps to more than ten, perhaps to more than twenty times the former number. So that there may be in Europe at present not only more than three times, but more than twenty or thirty times the quantity of plate which would have been in it, even in its present state of improvement, had the discovery of the American mines never been made. So far Europe has, no doubt, gained a real conveniency, though surely a very trifling one. The cheapness of gold and silver renders those metals rather less fit for the purposes of money than they were before. In order to make the same purchases, we must load ourselves with a great quantity of them, and carry about a shilling in our pocket where a groat would have done before. It is difficult to say which is most trifling, this inconveniency, or the opposite conveniency. Neither the one nor the other could have made any very essential change in the state of Europe. The discovery of America, however, certainly made a most essential one. By opening a new and inexhaustible market to all the commodities of Europe, it gave occasion to new divisions of labour and improvements of art, which, in the narrow circle of the ancient commerce, could never have taken place for want of a market to take off the greater part of their produce. The productive powers of labour were improved, and its produce increased in all the different countries of Europe, and together with it the real revenue and wealth of the inhabitants. The commodities of Europe were almost all new to America, and many of those of America were new to Europe. A new set of exchanges, therefore, began to take place which had never been thought of before, and which should naturally have proved as advantageous to the new, as it certainly did to the old continent. The savage injustice of the Europeans rendered an event, which ought to have been beneficial to all, ruinous and destructive to several of those unfortunate countries.

The discovery of a passage to the East Indies, by the Cape of Good Hope, which happened much about the same time, opened, perhaps, a still more extensive range to foreign commerce than even that of America, notwithstanding the greater distance. There were but two nations in America, in any respect superior to savages, and these were destroyed almost as soon as discovered. The rest were mere savages. But the empires of China, Indostan, Japan, as well as several others in the East Indies, without having richer mines of gold or silver, were in every other respect much richer, better cultivated, and more advanced in all arts and manufactures than either Mexico or Peru, even though we should credit, what plainly deserves no credit, the

exaggerated accounts of the Spanish writers, concerning the ancient state of those empires. But rich and civilized nations can always exchange to a much greater value with one another, than with savages and barbarians. Europe, however, has hitherto derived much less advantage from its commerce with the East Indies, than from that with America. The Portuguese monopolized the East India trade to themselves for about a century, and it was only indirectly and through them, that the other nations of Europe could either send out or receive any goods from that country. When the Dutch, in the beginning of the last century, began to encroach upon them, they vested their whole East India commerce in an exclusive company. The English, French, Swedes, and Danes, have all followed their example, so that no great nation in Europe has ever yet had the benefit of a free commerce to the East Indies. No other reason need be assigned why it has never been so advantageous as the trade to America, which, between almost every nation of Europe and its own colonies, is free to all its subjects. The exclusive privileges of those East India companies, their great riches, the great favour and protection which these have procured them from their respective governments, have excited much envy against them. This envy has frequently represented their trade as altogether pernicious, on account of the great quantities of silver, which it every year exports from the countries from which it is carried on. The parties concerned have replied, that their trade, by this continual exportation of silver, might, indeed, tend to impoverish Europe in general, but not the particular country from which it was carried on; because, by the exportation of a part of the returns to other European countries, it annually brought home a much greater quantity of that metal than it carried out. Both the objection and the reply are founded in the popular notion which I have been just now examining. It is, therefore, unnecessary to say any thing further about either. By the annual exportation of silver to the East Indies, plate is probably somewhat dearer in Europe than it otherwise might have been; and coined silver probably purchases a larger quantity both of labour and commodities. The former of these two effects is a very small loss, the latter a very small advantage; both too insignificant to deserve any part of the public attention. The trade to the East Indies, by opening a market to the commodities of Europe, or, what comes nearly to the same thing, to the gold and silver which is purchased with those commodities, must necessarily tend to increase the annual production of European commodities, and consequently the real wealth and revenue of Europe. That it has hitherto increased them so little, is probably owing to the restraints which it every-where labours under.

I thought it necessary, though at the hazard of being tedious, to examine at full length this popular notion that wealth consists in money, or in gold and silver. Money in common language, as I have already observed, frequently signifies wealth; and this ambiguity of expression has rendered this popular notion so familiar to us, that even they, who are convinced of its absurdity, are very apt to forget their own principles, and in the course of their reasonings to take it for granted as a certain and undeniable truth. Some of the best English writers upon commerce set out with observing, that the wealth of a country consists, not in its gold and silver only, but in its lands, houses, and consumable goods of all different kinds. In the course of their reasonings, however, the lands, houses, and consumable goods seem to slip out of their memory, and the strain of their argument frequently supposes that all wealth consists in gold and silver, and that to multiply those metals is the great object of national industry and commerce.

The two principles being established, however, that wealth consisted in gold and silver, and that those metals could be brought into a country which had no mines only by the balance of trade, or by export-

ing to a greater value than it imported; it necessarily became the great object of political oeconomy to diminish as much as possible the importation of foreign goods for home consumption, and to increase as much as possible the exportation of the produce of domestic industry. Its two great engines for enriching the country, therefore, were restraints upon importation, and encouragements to exportation.

The restraints upon importation were of two kinds.

First, Restraints upon the importation of such foreign goods for home consumption as could be produced at home, from whatever country they were imported.

Secondly, Restraints upon the importation of goods of almost all kinds from those particular countries with which the balance of trade was supposed to be disadvantageous.

Those different restraints consisted sometimes in high duties, and sometimes in absolute prohibitions.

Exportation was encouraged sometimes by drawbacks, sometimes by bounties, sometimes by advantageous treaties of commerce with foreign states, and sometimes by the establishment of colonies in distant countries.

Drawbacks were given upon two different occasions. When the home-manufactures were subject to any duty or excise, either the whole or a part of it was frequently drawn back upon their exportation; and when foreign goods liable to a duty were imported in order to be exported again, either the whole or a part of this duty was sometimes given back upon such exportation.

Bounties were given for the encouragement either of some beginning manufactures, or of such sorts of industry of other kinds as were supposed to deserve particular favour.

By advantageous treaties of commerce, particular privileges were procured in some foreign state for the goods and merchants of the country, beyond what were granted to those of other countries.

By the establishment of colonies in distant countries, not only particular privileges, but a monopoly was frequently procured for the goods and merchants of the country which established them.

The two sorts of restraints upon importation above-mentioned, together with these four encouragements to exportation, constitute the six principal means by which the commercial system proposes to increase the quantity of gold and silver in any country by turning the balance of trade in its favour.

The laudable motive of all these regulations, is to extend our own manufactures, not by their own improvement, but by the depression of those of all our neighbours, and by putting an end, as much as possible, to the troublesome competition of such odious and disagreeable rivals. Our master manufacturers think it reasonable, that they themselves should have the monopoly of the ingenuity of all their countrymen. Though by restraining, in some trades, the number of apprentices which can be employed at one time, and by imposing the necessity of a long apprenticeship in all trades, they endeavour, all of them, to confine the knowledge of their respective employments to as small a number as possible; they are unwilling, however, that any part of this small number should go abroad to instruct foreigners.

Consumption is the sole end and purpose of all production; and the interest of the producer ought to be attended to, only so far as it may be necessary for promoting that of the consumer. The maxim is so perfectly self-evident, that it would be absurd to attempt to prove it. But in the mercantile system, the interest of the consumer is almost constantly sacrificed to that of the producer; and it seems to consider production, and not consumption, as the ultimate end and object of all industry and commerce.

In the restraints upon the importation of all foreign commodities which can come into competition with those of our own growth, or manufacture, the interest of the home-consumer is evidently sacrificed to that of the producer. It is altogether for the benefit of the latter, that the former is obliged to pay that enhancement of price which this monopoly almost always occasions.

It is altogether for the benefit of the producer that bounties are granted upon the exportation of some of his productions. The home-consumer is obliged to pay, first, the tax which is necessary for paying the bounty, and secondly, the still greater tax which necessarily arises from the enhancement of the price of the commodity in the home market.

By the famous treaty of commerce with Portugal, the consumer is prevented by high duties from purchasing of a neighbouring country, a commodity which our own climate does not produce, but is obliged to purchase it of a distant country, though it is acknowledged, that the commodity of the distant country is of a worse quality than that of the near one. The home-consumer is obliged to submit to this inconveniency, in order that the producer may import into the distant country some of his productions upon more advantageous terms than he would otherwise have been allowed to do. The consumer, too, is obliged to pay, whatever enhancement in the price of those very productions, this forced exportation may occasion in the home market.

But in the system of laws which has been established for the management of our American and West Indian colonies, the interest of the home-consumer has been sacrificed to that of the producer with a more extravagant profusion than in all our other commercial regulations. A great empire has been established for the sole purpose of raising up a nation of customers who should be obliged to buy from the shops of our different producers, all the goods with which these could supply them. For the sake of that little enhancement of price which this monopoly might afford our producers, the home-consumers have been burdened with the whole expence of maintaining and defending that empire.

For this purpose, and for this purpose only, in the two last wars, more than two hundred millions have been spent, and a new debt of more than a hundred and seventy millions has been contracted over and above all that had been expended for the same purpose in former wars. The interest of this debt alone is not only greater than the whole extraordinary profit, which, it ever could be pretended, was made by the monopoly of the colony trade, but than the whole value of that trade, or than the whole value of the goods, which at an average have been annually exported to the colonies.

It cannot be very difficult to determine who have been the contrivers of this whole mercantile system; not the consumers, we may believe, whose interest has been entirely neglected; but the producers, whose interest has been so carefully attended to; and among this latter class our merchants and manufacturers have been by far the principal architects. In the mercantile regulations, which have been taken notice of in this chapter, the interest of our manufacturers has been most peculiarly attended to; and the interest, not so much of the consumers, as that of some other sets of producers, has been sacrificed to it.

Mercantilism as Unification

GUSTAV SCHMOLLER

Gustav Schmoller (1838–1917) was a prolific German economist who was professor successively at Halle, Strasbourg, and Berlin. Influenced by Friedrich List, Schmoller was the leader of the "younger school of German historical economists" who emphasized empirical research and the historical background of contemporary economic phenomena. He had a great influence on the development of economic history not only in Germany but elsewhere and was also active in public life. His account of *The Mercantile System and Its Historical Significance Illustrated Chiefly from Prussian History* forms part of his study of the economic policy of Frederick the Great.

THIS VERY TIME — the second half of the sixteenth century and the seventeenth century — was an epoch which gave every inducement for an economic transformation. The way was already clear, out of the narrow circle of the small territory into the larger union of forces possible only in the great state. An immeasurable horizon had been opened to the world's trade in India and America; the possession of spice colonies, and of the new gold and silver countries, promised measureless riches to those states that understood how to seize their share of the booty. But it was clear that for such purposes it was necessary to have powerful fleets, and either great trading companies or equivalent state organisations. At home, also, economic changes, of no less importance, took place. The new postal services created an altogether new system of communication. Bills of exchange, and the large exchange operations at certain fairs, together with the banks which were now making their appearance,

From Gustav Schmoller, *The Mercantile System and Its Historical Significance* (New York: Macmillan, 1914), 46–73. Reprinted by permission of Anne Ashley.

produced an enormous and far-reaching machinery of credit. The rise of the press gave birth to a new kind of public opinion, and to a crowd of newspapers which coöperated with the postal service in transforming the means of communication. Moreover, there now took place in the several countries a geographical division of labour, which broke up the old many-sidedness of town industry; here the woollen manufacture was grouping itself in certain neighbourhoods and around certain towns, there the linen manufacture; here the tanning trade, there the hardware trade. The old handicraft . . . began to convert itself into a domestic industry . . . ; the old staple trade, carried on in person by the travelling merchants, began to assume its modern shape with agents, commission dealers, and speculation.

These forces all converging impelled society to some large economic reorganisation on a broader basis, and pointed to the creation of national states with a corresponding policy. . . .

What, to each in its time, gave riches and superiority first to Milan, Venice, Florence, and Genoa; then, later, to Spain and Portugal; and now to Holland, France, and England, and, to some extent, to Denmark and Sweden, was a *state* policy in economic matters, as superior to the territorial as that had been to the municipal. Those states began to weave the great economic improvements of the time into their political institutions and policy, and to bring about an intimate relation between the one and the other. States arose, forming united, and therefore strong and wealthy, economic bodies, quite different from earlier conditions; in these, quite unlike earlier times, the state organisation assisted the national economy and this the state policy; and, quite unlike earlier times too, public finance served as the bond of union between political and economic life. It was not only a question of state armies, fleets, and civil services; it was a question rather of unifying systems of finance and economy which should encompass the forces of mil-

lions and whole countries, and give unity to their social life. There had always been great states; but they had been bound together neither by traffic nor by the organisation of labour nor by any other like forces. The question now was— with a great society divided into social classes widely different one from another and complicated by the division of labour — to bring about, as far as possible, on the basis of common national and religious feelings, a union for external defence and for internal justice and administration, for currency and credit, for trade interests and the whole economic life, which should be comparable with the achievements, in its time, of the municipal government in relation to the town and its environs. This was no mere fancy of the rulers; it was the innermost need of the higher civilisation itself that such enlarged and strengthened forms of social and economic community should come into existence. With the growing community in speech, art, and literature, with the growth of the spirit of nationality, with increasing communication and commerce, with money transactions and credit transactions becoming universal, the old mediæval forms of loose association no longer sufficed; and all the rigid local, corporate, class, and district organisations of an earlier time became intolerable hinderances to economic progress. Out of misery and conflict of every kind had arisen, in Spain as well as in France, in Holland as well as in England, the feeling of unity, the realisation of common interests; these it was, also, that prompted the stumbling search after new and wider forms of association. Herein economic and political interests went hand in hand. The stronger was the sense of nationality, the economic forces, the political power of any state, the more energetically did this movement get under way; for it meant a combining and organising of resources at home, even more than a measuring of them, when thus combined, with like creations across the frontier. The whole internal history of the seventeenth and eighteenth centuries, not only in Germany but everywhere else, is summed up in the opposition of the economic policy of the state to that of the town, the district, and the several Estates; the whole foreign history is summed up in the opposition to one another of the separate interests of the newly rising states, each of which sought to obtain and retain its place in the circle of European nations, and in that foreign trade which now included America and India. Questions of political power were at issue, which were, at the same time, questions of economic organisation. What was at stake was the creation of real *political* economies as unified organisms, the centre of which should be, not merely a state policy reaching out in all directions, but rather the living heartbeat of a united sentiment.

Only he who thus conceives of mercantilism will understand it; in its innermost kernel it is nothing but state making — not state making in a narrow sense, but state making and national-economy making at the same time; state making in the modern sense, which creates out of the political community an economic community, and so gives it a heightened meaning. The essence of the system lies not in some doctrine of money, or of the balance of trade; not in tariff barriers, protective duties, or navigation laws; but in something far greater: — namely, in the total transformation of society and its organisation, as well as of the state and its institutions, in the replacing of a local and territorial economic policy by that of the national state. With this accords the fact recently pointed out with regard to the literary history of the movement, that what is peculiar to all the mercantilist writers is not so much the regulations of trade which they propose for the increase of the precious metals as the stress they lay on the active circulation of money, especially within the state itself.

The struggle against the great nobility, the towns, the corporations, and provinces, the economic as well as political blending of these isolated groups into a larger whole, the struggle for uniform measures and coinage, for a well-ordered system of currency and credit, for uniform laws and uniform administration, for freer and more active traffic within the land — this it was which created a new division of labour, a new prosperity, and which liberated a thousand forces towards progress. As the territorial policy had rested on the overthrow of independent local and town policies, on the limitation and modification of local institutions upon the increasing strength of the general interests of the whole territory, so now there followed, for centuries, a struggle between state and district, between principality and province — a task which was doubly difficult in those cases where the state did not yet include the whole nation. This struggle was primarily an economic one; it had to do with the removal of all the old economic and financial institutions, and with the creation of new joint interests and of new and united institutions. It was a process which in Italy and Germany reached its full conclusion only in our own day; which in France was not quite finished in 1789; which even in Great Britain was not completed till late; and in the Republic of the United Netherlands halted midway in its course.

It is now to be noticed that it was the "enlightened," more or less despotic, monarchy of the seventeenth and eighteenth centuries by which this movement was initiated and pushed forward. Its whole activity centred in economic measures; its great administrative reforms were anti-municipal and anti-provincial, and aimed chiefly at the creation of larger economic organisms. With these princes mercantilist policy was not something subsidiary; all that they planned and performed necessarily took this direction.

*   *   *

If we pause for a while to consider this foreign and external economic policy of the European states of the seventeenth and eighteenth centuries — which it has hitherto been the custom to regard as the essential feature of the mercantile system — it is not, of course, our purpose to describe the details of its several forms. The general features of its regulations are well enough known. Difficulties were put in the way of the importation of manufactured goods; and their production and exportation were favoured by the prohibition of the export of raw materials, by bounties on export, and by commercial treaties. Encouragement was given to domestic shipping, to the fisheries, and to the coasting trade by restricting or forbidding foreign competition. Commerce with the colonies, and the supplying of them with European wares, was reserved for the mother country. The importation of colonial produce had to take place directly from the colony itself, and not by way of other European ports; and everywhere an attempt was made to establish *direct* trading relations by great privileged trading companies, and by state aid in manifold ways. England promoted the export of corn and the prosperity of agriculture at the same time by the payment of bounties; France hindered the export of corn for the benefit of industry; Holland, in its later days, sought to create very large stores of corn and a very free trade in corn, so as both to ensure a due domestic supply and to encourage trade. But, as we have already said, an account of these several measures would go beyond the purpose of this essay. The general features are known; the details have even yet not been subjected to due scientific investigation. Our only purpose here is to grasp the fundamental ideas of the system; which, naturally, found varying expression, here in high duties, there in low, here in the prevention, there in the encouragement of the corn trade. The thought pursued everywhere was this: as competition with other countries fluctuated up and down, to cast the weight of the power of the state into the scales of the balance in the way demanded in each case by national interests.

In proportion as the economic interests of whole states, after much agitation of public opinion, found a rallying-point in certain generally accepted postulates, there could not fail to arise the thought of a national policy, of protection by the state against the outside world, and of the support by the state of great national interests in their struggle with foreign countries. The conception of a national agriculture, of a national industry, of national shipping and fisheries, of national currency and banking systems, of a national division of labour, and of a national trade must have arisen before the need was felt of transforming old municipal and territorial institutions into national and state ones. But, as soon as that had taken place, it must have seemed a matter of course that the whole power of the state, in relation to other countries as well as at home, should be placed at the service of these collective interests; just as the political power of the towns and territories had served their municipal and district interests. The struggle for existence, in economic life in particular, as in social life in general, is necessarily carried on at all times by smaller or larger groups and communities. That will also be the case in all time to come. And the practice and theory of those times, answering, as they did, to this universal tendency, were nearer reality than the theory of Adam Smith; and so also were the main ideas of Frederick List.

We are not, however, concerned just now with this universal tendency; what we want is to understand the particular form in which it then expressed itself, and the reason for it; and why it could, in later times, give way so far before other tendencies.

The great states of an earlier time display no commercial policy in the style of the mercantile system, not because the Utopia of a purely individualistic economic life possessed more reality then than later, but because they were not united economic bodies; as soon as they became such, the inheritance of such economic bodies as had previously existed, and, above all, of the town policy, passed over to them. It was not because money and money payments or industry or trade suddenly played an altogether new rôle in the days of Cromwell and Colbert, that it occurred to people to guide the course of exportation and importation and colonial trade, and to subject them to governmental control. On the contrary, it was because just then, out of the earlier smaller communities, great national communities had grown up, whose power and significance rested on their psychological and social concert, that they began to imitate, not what Charles V. had done in Spain, but what all towns and territories of earlier times had done, from the Tyre and Sidon, from Athens and Carthage onward; to carry over what Pisa and Genoa, Florence and Venice, and the German Hanse towns had done in their time to the broad basis of whole states and nations. The whole idea and doctrine of the Balance of Trade, as it then arose, was only the secondary consequence of a conception of economic processes which grouped them according to states. Just as up to this time attention had been fixed on the exportation from and importation to particular towns and territories, so now people tried to grasp in their minds the trade of the state as a whole, and to sum it up in such a way as to arrive at a better understanding of it and at some practical conclusion. Such a grouping and combination were very evidently suggested in a country like England, where, on account of its insular position and the moderate size of the land, the national economy had early displayed its exports and imports, its supply of money and of the precious metals, as a connected whole to the eye of the observer.

All economic and political life rests upon psychical mass-movements, mass-sentiments, and mass-conceptions, gravitating around certain centres. That age could begin to think and act in the spirit of free trade, which had left so far behind it the toilsome work of national development that it regarded its best results as matters of course, and forgot the struggle they had cost; an age which, with cosmopolitan sentiments, with great institutions and interests of international traffic, with a humanised international law, and an individualist literature everywhere diffused, was already beginning to live in the ideas and tendencies of a world economy. . . . The seventeenth century had just managed to fight its way up from local sentiment to national sentiment; international law as yet scarcely existed. The old bonds which had held together Catholic states had been broken; all the intellectual movement of the time centred in the new national life; and the stronger and sounder beat the pulse of that life, the more it felt its individuality, the more inevitable was it that it should bar itself against the world outside with a harsh egoism. Each new political community that forms itself must be carried along by a strong and exclusive feeling of community; these are the roots of its strength. The struggle for self-sufficiency and independence is as natural to it as the spirit of violent rivalry which hesitates at nothing in order to come up with, to surpass, and to crush the rivals in whom it always sees enemies. It was the law of autarchy by which the commercial policy of those times was exclusively guided. The endeavour after autarchy naturally shews itself in an especially violent and one-sided form in the youth of nations.

The doctrine of the natural harmony of the economic interests of all states is just as false as the opinion then entertained that an advantage to one state is always a disadvantage to another. The latter was an opinion which not only had its roots in the earlier stubborn struggles between towns and territories, but was strengthened just at this time by the circumstance that the possession of colonies, of the Indian Spice Islands, and of the silver mines of America had fallen to the several nations only as the result of war and bloodshed. It seemed unavoidable that one nation should have to recede when another pressed in. In reality, all social bodies, and therefore economic bodies among them — at first towns and districts, and afterwards nations and states — stand to one another in a double relation; a relation of action and reaction by which they mutually supplement one another, and a relation of dependence, exploitation, and struggle for supremacy. The latter is the original one; and only slowly, in the course of centuries and millenniums, is the antagonism softened. Even to-day the great economic Powers seek to utilise their economic superiority in all their international relations, and to retain weaker nations in dependence; even to-day any half-civilised nation or tribe, among whom the English or French establish themselves, is in danger, first, of a sort of slavery for debt and an unfavourable balance of trade, and, following closely in the wake, of political annexation and economic exploitation — though this, indeed, may turn into an economic education for it.

In the seventeenth and eighteenth centuries the relations, and especially the economic relations, between states were particularly hostile and harsh, because the new economico-political creations were for the first time trying their strength, and because it was the first time that such considerable political forces were available for the pursuit of commercial, agricultural, and industrial ends — forces which might seem, if only properly employed, to promise untold wealth to every state. In all ages history has been wont to treat national power and national wealth as sisters; perhaps they were never so closely associated as then. The temptation to the greater states of that time to use their political power for conflict with their economic competitors, and when they could, for their destruction, was too great for them not to succumb time after time, and either to set international law at naught or twist it to their purposes. Commercial competition, even in times nominally of peace, degenerated into a state of undeclared hostility: it plunged nations into one war after another, and gave all wars a turn in the direction of trade, industry, and colonial gain, such as they never had before or after.

*   *   *

The long wars, each lasting several years, or even decades, which fill the whole period from 1600 to 1800 and have economic objects as their main aim; the open declaration by the Grand Alliance in 1689 that their object was the destruction of French commerce; the prohibition by the Allies of all trade, even by neutrals, with France, without the slightest regard to international law; all this shews the spirit of the time in its true light. The national passion of economic rivalry had been raised to such a height that it was only in wars like these that it could find its full expression and satisfaction. To be content, in the intermediate years of peace, to carry on the conflict with prohibition, tariffs, and navigation laws instead of with sea fights; to give, as they did, in these years of peace, somewhat more attention to the infant voice of international law than in time of war — this was in itself a moderating of international passion.

The very idea of international law is a protest against the excesses of national rivalry. All international law rests on the idea that the several states and nations form, from the moral point of view, one community. Since the men of Europe had lost the feeling of community that had been created by the Papacy and Empire, they had been seeking for some other theory which might serve to support it; and this they found in the reawakening "law of nature." But the particular ideas for which in the first instance men strove, and for which they sought arguments *pro et contra* in the law of nature, were mainly products of the economic and commercial struggle then proceeding.

Inasmuch as the states that were the first to obtain colonies on a large scale, Spain and Portugal, had secured from the Pope a partition of the whole oceanic world, and its designation by him as their exclusive property, the law of nature, when it made its appearance, put forward the doctrine of *Mare liberum*. But while in this way Hugo Grotius in 1609 created a legal justification for his Dutch fellow-countrymen in pushing their way into the old possessions of the Portuguese and Spaniards, the English maintained the opposite theory of *Mare clausum,* and of the exclusive lordship of England over the British seas, in order to free their necks from the competition of the Dutch in navigation and the fisheries. Denmark appealed to its sovereignty of the sea as a justification for its oppressive tolls at the Sound; and the other Baltic powers sought, on the same ground, to forbid the Great Elector to build a fleet. The great principle of the freedom of the sea did, indeed, slowly gain general currency; but at first each nation only recognised the particular theory that promised it some advantage.

Almost all the wars of the time were waged in the name of the European "Balance." And who will deny that this idea had its justification, and that it laid the foundation for the peaceful future of a great community of states? But, at first, it was a mere phrase taken from international law, and used to justify every caprice on the part of the Great Powers, every intervention in the relations, and every interference with the fate of the small states: it was the cloak which hid the silent conspiracy of the western Powers to prevent the rise of a new Power, like the Prussian, and to keep its trade and its whole economic life in the bonds of dependence.

The gradual growth of the milder principle, more favourable to the small states, which is summed up in the phrase "free ships, free goods," out of the mediæval principle found in the *Consolato del Mare,* which allowed the confiscation of the enemy's property even on friendly neutral ships, is one of the great gains in international law in the eighteenth century. But England has never accommodated herself to it, and has, with unheard-of assurance, and with decisions of the Court of Admiralty about prizes which can have been determined by nothing but national egoism, succeeded in injuring the trade of neutrals everywhere, in time of war, even when it could not destroy it. Büsch shewed, in 1797, that of the last one hundred and forty-four years England had spent sixty-six in the most sanguinary naval wars. They had all been more or less concerned, on the one side, with the conquest of colonies by force of arms, on the other, with the destruction of the neutral trade, *i.e.,* the trade of the smaller states.

The blows of the English are nearest to us in time; they have also vitally affected Germany; and, accordingly, we are inclined — measuring with the standard of today — to condemn them most. On the whole, however, they were naught else than what all the more powerful commercial powers allowed themselves in their treatment of the weaker. And although we condemn the whole period for excesses in the politico-commercial struggle, and see everywhere much injustice and error mingled with it, yet we must allow that passions and blunders such as these were the necessary concomitants of the new state policy, of the developing national economies; we must feel that those states and governments are not to be praised which did not pursue such a policy, but those who knew how to apply it in a more skillful, energetic, and systematic way than others. For it was precisely those governments which understood how to put the might of their fleets and admiralties, the apparatus of customs laws and navigation laws, with rapidity, boldness, and clear purpose, at the service of the economic interests of the nation and state, which obtained thereby the lead in the struggle and in riches and industrial prosperity. Even if they frequently went too far, and were led by theories that were only half true, and gathered riches by violence and exploitation, yet, at the same time, they gave the economic life of their people its necessary basis of power, and a corresponding impulse to its economic movement; they furnished the national striving with great aims; they created and liberated forces which were absent or slumbered in the states they outstripped. And it was natural that what in these struggles was brutal and unjust should be lost to sight in each nation in the glow of national and economic success. We can understand that the several peoples asked only whether a Cromwell or a Colbert on the whole furthered national prosperity, and not whether he did injustice to foreigners in some one point. And historical justice does not demand more: it gives its approbation to systems of government which help a people to reach the great goal of national greatness and moral unity at a given time and with the means of that time, at home and abroad; systems, moreover, which have redeemed the harshness of national and state egoism as regards neighbouring peoples, by a model administration at home.

Mercantilism as Power

WILLIAM CUNNINGHAM

Archdeacon William Cunningham (1849–1919) was educated at Edinburgh and Tübingen, where he came under the influence of the German historical economists. One of the founders of English economic history, he was a prolific writer. He is now chiefly remembered for his *Growth of English Industry and Commerce*, first published in 1882. In addition to being a historian, he was a busy and distinguished churchman.

THE GREAT discoveries of the last decades of the fifteenth century effected a revolution in the whole trade of the world, for they opened communications between the most distant parts, and thus laid the foundations for the great international commerce of present times. Mediæval, like earlier European trade, centred in the cities of the Mediterranean; there were streams of traffic by the Russian rivers and the Danube, which led towards the Baltic and to South Germany, but the great centres of commerce and industry were on the shores of the Mediterranean; the citizens of Genoa and Venice were the chief agents in carrying on the traffic between East and West. But when the Cape of Good Hope was successfully rounded by the Portuguese, an entirely new prospect was opened to European traders; they could make their way to India direct, instead of submitting to the exactions of intermediaries in Alexandria and elsewhere; the great stream of commerce between East and West was at once directed from the Levant to the Atlantic, and the Portuguese became for a time the chief trading people of the world. Partly at all events in the hope of sharing in this lucrative trade, Columbus planned the voyages which led him to the West India Islands, and Cabot found his way to the coast of North America. A little later, according to the ordinarily accepted view, a Portuguese expedition to the East was driven out of its course, and this led to the discovery of Brazil; and from this time onwards Lisbon bore away the palm from the Italian cities and became the great commercial depôt for Western Europe.

Henry VII was too parsimonious to seize the opportunities which were offered him and to take a leading part in this age of discovery; perhaps the English colonial empire was all the stronger because it grew

From William Cunningham, *Growth of English Industry and Commerce*, I (Cambridge: University Press, 4th ed., 1905), 473–83.

so slowly; the immediate effects on English commerce were small, but none the less the events of this time really form the great epoch in English commercial history. Far from the Mediterranean, English merchants had taken little part in the trade of the world; they sold English products and catered for English tastes, but they had not had any opportunity of acting as intermediaries and carrying goods to their own depôts to be distributed thence to other nations. From the Tudor times onwards English trade assumed this character, and with ever-increasing success; in the present day by far the larger part of the trade of the world is carried on in English ships, and London is a depôt for the trade of all nations. England had only been on a side-eddy before, but the discoveries of the fifteenth century placed her on the main stream; and though the immediate results were small, English enterprise took a new character with most far-reaching effects.

The change lies far deeper than any mere modification of the political life of the country, for it affected the world as a whole, and England as one of the family of nations arising in Christendom; it is a striking instance of the sudden removal of a limit imposed by physical conditions, and of the extraordinary advance which enterprise is ready to make when thus set free. It has no parallel but in the mechanical inventions of the last hundred years; in both cases advancing knowledge removed barriers which seemed to be insuperable. The limit lay of course, as always, not in any material obstacle which was removed by some physical change, but in the want of that knowledge and skill which at length enabled men to grapple with the difficulty and overcome it. There is no absolute limit to the advance which man may ultimately make; though there is in every age a relative limit, not set by physical nature, but corresponding to the limitations of human skill and energy at that time. . . .

Before this commercial revolution occurred, industry and commerce had been considered almost entirely with reference to the internal condition of the country; commercial policy was affected by the facilities for collecting customs and the prospect of increasing them, and by the expectation of providing plenty, or of securing employment for the people. Local interests had gradually fallen more and more into the background, and parliament legislated for the prosperity of England as a whole; but at length men came to see that if this was to be preserved, they must take a still wider survey. We have already traced the growth of the idea of a national interest; in modern times, this conception has been consciously grasped and has dominated all commercial policy. Our statesmen have considered the condition and progress of England not by itself, but relatively to that of other nations; what they sought was not mere progress within their own land, for they wished to prosper relatively to other nations. They were not satisfied to aim at maintaining some standard of comfort, they desired to exercise an influence upon the peoples of the world. In fact the object of their ambition was to increase the power of the nation, and greater power implies a greater relative advance; greater power could be obtained by inflicting loss on others as well as by attaining positive gain for England; it has distinct reference to a relative condition. If we discuss whether England is a more powerful maritime realm now than ten years ago, we must consider not merely what the fleet was and is, but what other fleets were and are; we may have bigger ships and better armed, but we are not stronger for offence and defence if we have merely considered the excellence, and not the relative superiority of our own navy. The one leading idea of policy which caused so much national rivalry, and led statesmen to attach so much importance to the maintenance of the "balance" in Europe, was this aspiration after national power, or relative superiority.

It was brought out into stronger relief by the rise of other nationalities in Europe — the consolidation of Spain under Ferdinand and Isabella, and the recovering strength of the French monarchy; and also by the great struggles which occupied the sixteenth century. The division of Europe in regard to the papal pretensions, the religious passions which they called into being, and the eager desire to partake in the expected treasure of the New World, aroused the bitterest feelings of jealousy between rival nations.

The keen national feeling which was thus evoked, and the desire to strengthen the power of England against all her rivals, affected the commercial and industrial legislation in every particular; on every hand private tastes and personal convenience had to give way to the patriotic duty of strengthening the nation. It was thus that men were required by law to eat fish all through Lent and twice a week throughout the year; they might not like fish, but by buying it they helped to encourage fishermen and thus indirectly to keep up a school for seamanship. Time-honoured sentiment had preferred that the dead should be wrapped in linen, but public policy demanded that this sentiment should be set aside and that woollen should be used. And as in these matters, so in everything else; current opinion demanded that private interest should be set aside, at once, in favour of an apparent public gain. How far the gain which accrued to the power of the country was real may be discussed below; that there was a distinct loss to individuals from the enactments no one would have denied. It was admitted that the planters were hampered by the navigation act, and the Englishmen who had established grazing farms in Ireland suffered from the laws against importing cattle; there was a loss of their wealth, and a decrease of the aggregate wealth to that extent. This was obvious long before the time of Adam Smith; but parliament had no scruple in doing these injuries, because they believed, rightly or wrongly, that it was necessary to sacrifice the interests of some individuals for the sake of increasing the shipping and maintaining the wealth which was available for national defence. They may have been

right or may have been wrong; in some matters they certainly made grave errors of judgment, but they were not ignorant of the bearing of the policy they pursued. Current sentiment has changed so much in regard to this matter that it is very difficult for us to understand the attitude which was generally taken in the sixteenth century by public opinion; the one reiterated complaint which we meet with on all sides is that men were seeking their private lucre and singular advantage, without having due care for the prosperity of the community. Artisans who withdrew from the pressure of burgh rates and the restrictions of craft gilds, landlords who raised their rents, miners who did their work in the easiest way, capitalists who asked for a definite return on their capital, were all branded as the victims of covetousness, not merely by preachers and writers, but in public documents.

The politicians of the sixteenth, seventeenth and greater part of the eighteenth century were agreed in trying to regulate all commerce and industry, so that the power of England relatively to other nations might be promoted; and in carrying out this aim they had no scruple in trampling on private interests of every kind. The main principles of the scheme of policy which dominated in England during this long period have been sketched above, but it may be convenient to repeat them a little more fully, as they furnish the framework on which the facts of the succeeding periods in the national life may be most clearly exhibited.

Power depends on (*a*) the accumulation of Treasure, (*b*) the development of Shipping, and (*c*) the maintenance of an effective Population.

(*a*) The accumulation of Treasure, in a country which has no mines, depends on the proper management of commerce, whether by (1) making regulations for the flow of the precious metals and the exchanges, or (2) by making regulations for the export and import of commodities. From this point of view the volume of transactions is much less important as a sign of prosperity than the nature of the trade that is being carried on.

(b) A strong navy was obviously necessary for defence, and with this purpose it was desirable to encourage the employment of English ships; hence we have a whole series of navigation acts, while attention was also directed to measures for procuring the materials for shipbuilding and necessary naval stores. It was also felt to be a matter of the first importance that we should encourage the fishing trade, as that was the best school for seamen.

Subject to the restrictions about the kind of trade and its bearing on treasure, the increase of the volume of trade was important, as it not only gave a larger sum in customs but also stimulated the development of shipping. Hence there was a preference for distant trade over coasting trade, as it gave more employment to ships, while the commodities of distant lands were often things that could not be produced at home. On the other hand, the planting of new trades in England, the development of our industry, and the retention of all the arts in which we excelled, enabled us to dispense with purchases from rival lands and gave us more products which we might sell in the markets we frequented. This also tended to give employment to our own peo-

ple and so to maintain an effective population. Hence arose all the attempts to regulate industry; it did not itself directly promote power, but it could be so managed as to give a stimulus to the accumulation of treasure, and lead to the development of commerce as well as provide favourable conditions for the population.

(c) This last object depended most immediately and directly on the food supply. Sufficient corn could be most easily secured by the encouragement of tillage, though the fisheries were also an important source of supply; tillage also gave the kind of employment which was most favourable for the maintenance of a healthy and vigorous race, accustomed to outdoor sports and likely to offer the best material for forming a military force.

The end in view was Power; this was furthered by attention to Treasure, Shipping and Population; while these objects could only be attained by the careful regulation of Industry and Tillage. Such in brief is the *rationale* of the so-called Mercantile System, which had been gradually coming into operation since the time of Richard II, and which survived with much vigour in some of its parts till Cobden and Bright completed the revolution in English policy.

III. HECKSCHER AND HIS CRITICS

Mercantilism—A Theory of Society

ELI HECKSCHER

Eli Heckscher (1879–1952) was the most distinguished economic historian that Sweden has so far produced. He was active both as a teacher and in public life, but his most fruitful work was done after his appointment as research professor in economic history in the Stockholm School of Economics. His most influential work is *Mercantilism*, but his best was probably his study of the economic and social history of Sweden. To Heckscher more than any other man, the current discussion of mercantilism owes its origin.

MERCANTILISM, originally a term of opprobrium, lacks the clear cut meaning of an expression coined for purely scientific purposes. Used sporadically by the French physiocrats, the term was brought into general currency through Adam Smith, who devoted about one fourth of *The Wealth of Nations* to a relentless criticism of what he termed "the commercial or mercantile system." His attack started with the views of money which he attributed to the mercantilist writers; but the greater part of his discussion referred to commercial policy and consequently treated mercantilism as a system of protection. More than a century later in 1884 a greatly different use of the word was introduced by Gustav Schmoller in his essay, *Das Merkantilsystem in seiner historischen Bedeutung*. In Schmoller's opinion mercantilism was essentially a policy of economic unity — to a large extent independent of particular economic tenets — expressing the efforts of territorial princes, German in the first place, to overcome the disruption caused by mediaeval conditions. In England at about the same time William

Cunningham in *The Growth of English Industry and Commerce* (1882) viewed mercantilism still differently as the expression of a striving after economic power for political purposes manifesting itself particularly in England. The discordance between these views was principally due to a confusion between the ends and means of economic policy; each of them pointed to something of fundamental importance in the development of economic activities and ideas in the period between the Middle Ages and the industrial revolution.

If one considers mercantilism first as a system of national economic unity, it is quite clear that there was an enormous task awaiting the rulers of most continental states at the end of the Middle Ages. Under feudalism independent petty rulers and even quite ordinary private landowners had usurped the power of the state, harassing and impeding trade and industry and laying both under contribution for their own benefit. Among the numerous manifestations of this tendency the most important was perhaps the almost endless confusion caused throughout Europe by

From the *Encyclopedia of the Social Sciences* (New York, Macmillan), X, 333–39. By permission of the publishers.

33

tolls on rivers and highways as well as by the impediments placed on trade between different provinces. An English chronicler, William Wykes, speaking of conditions in the late thirteenth century referred to *furiosa teutonicorum insania,* "the wild madness of the Germans"; but the condition was quite as widespread in France. On all the great rivers there were separate tolls for each ten or at most fifteen kilometers, which the trader had to pay in succession. The work of unification necessitated the doing away with all this and the creation of national customs systems.

In England, where very little of this confusion had ever existed, unification was achieved in the course of the thirteenth century; but on the continent progress was slow and very little was accomplished before the nineteenth century. By far the most important success was scored by Colbert in France through his tariff of 1664. This tariff did away with most of the duties separating from one another the provinces constituting the so-called *cinq grosses fermes;* something like three eighths of the French monarchy was thus made into a single customs territory. But this was in respect only of interprovincial customs. With regard to river and highway tolls Colbert was able to achieve very little; and the customs boundaries between the rest of the provinces he left entirely untouched, with the result that areas conquered about the middle of the sixteenth century were treated as foreign territory from a customs point of view until the French Revolution. Nevertheless, the French tariff of 1664 was almost the only important measure in the direction of customs unification carried out under mercantilism, although Colbert for one was quite aware of the connection between the work of unification and mercantilist aims in the fields of money, foreign trade and colonization.

Throughout this period the towns had a well thought out and surprisingly consistent policy, which also tended to split up the unity of a state's territory. Each town attempted to subject the adjacent country-side to its control and to hamper in every possible way the trade of competing towns. Mercantilist policy involved the substitution of a scheme which would give the whole territory the benefits that each town had tried to arrogate to itself. The direction of town policy need not necessarily be changed, but its scope must be enlarged from a municipal to a national field.

One such victory of national policy is to be recorded in the famous act of Queen Elizabeth of England — or of her minister William Cecil, Lord Burghley — the Statute of Artificers . . . and Apprentices (1562). Besides Colbert's unifying tariff of 1664 it is perhaps the only successful achievement of mercantilism in the field of economic unity. Based upon legislation which went back to the Black Death, it created a consistent national system of regulation of internal trade and industry in town and country alike, which lasted on paper until the early nineteenth century (1813–14). The positive importance of this measure consisted in its national scope. There was nothing in it favoring the towns at the expense of the countryside, and it did nothing to perpetuate the craft guilds, the typical products of town policy and economy. The guilds were thus prevented from becoming a component part of the trade regulatory system, a circumstance which contributed to weakening the hold of the mediaeval order. Otherwise the factors working for economic change had little relation to mercantilist measures, in England as in other countries. The statesmen of later Tudor and earlier Stuart times made unusually successful attempts to revive the old system of regulation, but that very fact worked in the direction of undermining it when the parliamentary party became victorious.

The importance of this development becomes clear when the French parallel is studied. For in France mercantilism accepted and tried to nationalize the mediaeval system. By the edicts of 1581, 1597 and 1673 the guilds were made compulsory throughout the country even outside the towns; and although these measures came far from achieving their purpose, the whole mediaeval system of regulation was given through them a new and wider lease of life. At the same time the craft guilds remained as exclusively local as they had ever been, so that labor and industry were prevented from flowing freely between the different parts of the country. This was probably one of the reasons why the industrial revolution began in England instead of France. French mercantilism saw the rise of a very extensive civil service engaged in industrial as well as other types of supervision, while England had not even the semblance of such a body. The famous *règlements,* issued at an ever increasing rate from the time of Colbert onward, all perpetuated the mediaeval treatment of industry. A great deal was thus achieved in the perfecting of production on the old lines; but the development of the charactertistic aspect of modern industry, mass production for mass consumption, was hampered rather than furthered through the most effective and consistent forms of mercantilist regulation.

The situation was somewhat different in the field of international trade and business organization in general. On the double foundation of private partnerships, mostly of Italian origin, and mediaeval merchant guilds there arose a network of new business corporations, of which the English were more important for later developments, although the Dutch were at one time more powerful. The distinguishing feature of the so-called regulated companies in England which proved so remarkably successful in Atlantic, Mediterranean and Baltic trade was that each merchant traded for himself, although under the rules of the company and with the use of its organization. These chartered companies paved the way for the joint stock company, the direct ancestor of the most important of all modern forms of business organization, the corporation. For the history of mercantilism the important question is to what extent these development were due to mercantilist policy. In Portugal, Spain and France the chartered companies and the organization of foreign trade and colonization in general were the outcome of state initiative; but in Holland and England, the two important countries in this field, the trading companies were created by private merchants. The state confined itself to giving them more or less extensive privileges, for which they often had to pay dearly, one of which was the preventing of others from use of the more advanced joint stock form of organization. In 1719 the English Parliament passed the Bubble Act, which was intended to check a general growth of company organization and may have achieved at least part of its object. Altogether it is far from clear that the remarkable development of company organization was to any great extent due to mercantilist policy in those countries where it was most important.

The results of mercantilist activity in overcoming the disruption caused by mediaeval conditions were thus rather limited. The laissez faire era may even be considered its executor in this respect. Through the influence of the French Revolution in other countries as well as in France and through the rise of new ideas in the field of economic policy the end of the eighteenth and the first half of the nineteenth century saw changes introduced without much difficulty for which mercantilist statesmen had been striving in vain for several hundred years.

But efforts in the direction of economic unity were only the frame of mercantilist policy. The next question must be, for what purposes mercantilist statesmen wanted to use the resources of a unified state. The answer is, principally for strengthening the powers of the state in its competition with other states. While the mediaeval conception of the object of human effort was the salvation of human souls and while economic liberalism, or laissez faire, aimed at the temporal welfare of individuals, mercantilist statesmen and writers saw in the subjects of the state means to an end, and the end was the power of the state itself. The foremost exponent of this aspect of mercantilism was Colbert; but he had counterparts everywhere. The British navigation laws as well as the old colonial system were its most lasting results. Combined with a static view of economic life this doctrine was responsible for the perpetual commercial wars of the later seventeenth and the eighteenth century, culminating in Napoleon's Continental System and the British Orders in Council of 1807. For if power was the object of economic policy and if the total fund of economic power was given once for all, the only method of benefiting one's own country was to take something away from someone else. Nobody has pointed this out with greater logical incisiveness than Colbert; and, conversely, David Hume in his criticism of mercantilism turned against just this "jealousy of trade."

It soon becomes clear, however, that the characteristic features of this policy resulted less from the striving after power in itself than from the views of its exponents as to the proper means for attaining power or prosperity. Only at this point do we reach the real economic import of mercantilism, what constitutes it an economic tenet and what reveals the fundamental differences between mercantilists and their predecessors as well as their successors. Adam Smith, for example, was entirely in accord with mercantilist aims when he wrote that "defence is of much greater importance than opulence"; the only difference was that he laid much less stress than earlier writers upon that aspect of the problem. The extent to which mercantilists and laissez faire economists were in agreement with regard to ends is suggested by a comparison of the title of Adam Smith's famous work with that of the most important book belonging to German mercantilistic literature, the *Politischer Discurs von den eigentlichen Ursachen des Aufund Abnehmens der Städt, Länder und Republicken*, by Johann Joachim Becher (Frankfort 1668, 2nd ed. 1673). Only slight shades of meaning distinguish this title from that of the bible of laissez faire. But in their view of

the relations between means and ends two books could hardly be more unlike. There lies the most distinctive feature of mercantilism.

The mercantilist conception of what was to a country's advantage centered on two closely allied aspects of economic life — the supply of commodities and of money. These doctrines are best considered separately.

It was possible to regard commodities in a purely neutral way as something to be bought or sold and neither in preference. This was the merchant's point of view; as a German author (Laspeyres) has well said with regard to the Dutch: "The merchant was a free trader in every direction; he wanted no limitation of exports, in order to send out large quantities of goods; no obstacles to imports, in order to take in large quantities; finally no hampering of transit trade, in order both to import and export large quantities." This was what might be called the staple policy of the mediaeval towns, developed first in Italy and Germany, that of drawing trade in both directions to the town itself and away from all competitors. A late but important outcome of this was the old colonial system making the metropolis an *entrepôt* of colonial trade, an idea which culminated in the British Orders in Council of 1807. Important as this tendency was during many centuries of European history it could, however, never triumph completely as it appealed only to a small minority in every community. Instead two other and entirely opposing views came in succession to dominate commercial policy.

The prevalent mediaeval idea had been that a community should aim at the securing of plenty, as Francis Bacon pointed out in his *History of Henry VII* in saying that that monarch was "bowing the ancient policy of this estate from the consideration of plenty to the consideration of power." The result was the setting up of obstacles to exports and the facilitating of imports. Throughout the Middle Ages export prohibitions were innumerable in most countries, while import prohibitions were very scarce. Commercial treaties aimed at securing imports, exports being granted as a favor; in one case it was even required that goods manufactured from raw materials set free for export should be sent back.

It was in criticisms of the prevalence of export prohibitions that the new attitude which was to become typical of mercantilism first found utterance. In *A Discourse of the Common Weal of Thys Realm of England* (1581; ed. by E. Lammond, Cambridge, Eng. 1893), probably written in 1549 by John Hales, one of the most intelligent of mercantilist writers, it was shown at some length and quite clearly how the prevention of exports counteracts its own aim through hampering the production of. the commodities in question, while free exports would result in increased production. Mercantilist thought here showed an advance over mediaeval ideas in its ability to take a long view and to disprove the belief that consumers profit by everything which creates monetary plenty. The same trend of thought appears in a well known sentence by Thomas Mun, in *England's Treasure by Forraign Trade* (reprinted Oxford 1928), written about the end of the 1620's and published posthumously in 1664. Referring to export of bullion he writes: "For if we only behold the actions of the husbandman in the seed-time, when he casteth away much good corn into the ground, we will rather accompt him a mad man than a husbandman; but when we consider his labours in the harvest, which is the end of his endeavours, we find the worth and plentiful encrease of his actions." This view of economic life reappeared in the nineteenth century in the teachings of Friedrich List as well as in the "infant industry argument" of John Stuart Mill.

But it did not in itself mean a changed attitude toward the supply of commodities. Mercantilists went much further, however, turning against "a dead stock called plenty," not only for the moment but for the long run period. They came to look upon a plentiful supply of commodities within a country with as great disfavor as mediaeval statesmen had regarded a depletion of commodities. The great object became to *décharger le royaume de ses marchandises*, stimulating exports and hampering imports by every conceivable means. Only thus was a country believed to become "rich"; Sir William Petty characteristically wrote in 1662, and Sir Josiah Child repeated a few years later, that Ireland, "exporting more than it imports, doth yet grow poorer to a paradox" — the opposite result was considered the only natural one. According to this view production must be stimulated to the utmost, but products kept out and sent away. The most difficult problem was the relative treatment of the different factors of production. A natural solution was to retain goods in accordance with their importance to production or with their character as raw materials; but these points of view were very largely discordant and a consistent policy was therefore impossible. On the other hand, it was possible to find a solution with regard to one of the prerequisites of production; namely, labor, as that was not "produced." The result was encouragement of population increase, of child labor and of low wages as a method of stimulating production and increasing the competing power of a country.

It goes without saying that the mercantilist treatment of the supply of commodities was not the outcome of theoretical speculation, although such speculation later developed. How far back the policy of hampering imports went it is difficult to say, but the first known traces of the new policy date from the beginning of the thirteenth century in the towns of north Italy, especially Venice. It passed to the Netherlands about the middle of the following century and to France and England a century later, Edward IV being perhaps the first English ruler wholeheartedly to embrace protection.

Mercantilism in the sense of a policy and doctrine of protection represents the most original contribution of the period in question to economic policy and the one which has retained more sway over men's

minds than any other. Various causes contributed to this great change from mediaeval ideas; the most influential apparently
was the growing importance of money
economy. So long as commodities were
mostly exchanged against one another, it
was clear to the meanest capacities that
nothing could be gained by receiving little
in exchange for what you gave away but
quite the reverse. When, however, all exchange transactions were overlaid by the
cloak of money, the workings of economic
life became infinitely more difficult to understand; and then it was easy to believe
that commodities were a nuisance and a
danger, especially as a cause of unemployment. Although this view was first held
with regard to manufactures it spread over
the whole economic field, in England coming from a comparatively early date to embrace even food products. As a money economy still survives, it is natural that the
mercantilist view of commodities should
also have survived when the rest of mercantilism lost its influence, although the
ruthless consistency of laissez faire obliterated this too for a short time from men's
minds.

So far no mention has been made of the
mercantilist views of money. In the opinion
of Adam Smith and his followers, however,
the real gist of mercantilist doctrine was
expressed in the statement "that wealth
consists in money, or in gold and silver."
From this point of view mercantilist insistence upon an excess of exports over imports — the flow of bullion and money
omitted from consideration — was explained
as inability to distinguish between money
and wealth. It is easy to find in mercantilist
literature and state papers an almost unlimited number of utterances supporting that
interpretation. But the fact that in recent
times the policy of protection has retained
or regained its sway, although little is now
heard about the necessity for an inflow of
precious metals, indicates that protection is
the more fundamental tenet. In the mercantilistic period, however, the two cooper-
ated harmoniously.

The differences between an earlier and a
later policy with regard to exports of money
have led to the drawing of a distinction
between bullionists . . . and mercantilists
proper. The former wanted to prohibit the
outflow of bullion, while the latter brought
forward a theory of the balance of trade
and saw in an excess of exports over imports of commodities the only possible
means of increasing the monetary stock of
a country without mines of precious metals.
The distinction was certainly important not
only for economic policy but perhaps even
more as an expression of a general concept
of society; but it is also true that both
schools were in agreement as to the benefits
of a large stock of money. Such a view is
indeed very old; what mercantilism did was
to bring the rest of economic policy into
harmony with it and to elaborate many ingenious although usually mistaken theories
to fortify it. The mercantilist theory of
money was elaborated principally by a host
of English writers in the seventeenth century, foremost among whom were Thomas
Mun, Sir William Petty, Sir Josiah Child,
John Locke and Charles Davenant; outside
England there were few besides Bernardo
Davanzati, Antonio Serra and Jean Bodin,
the German writers contributing little of
an original character in this field.

It is of course a travesty of the real opinion of these writers to say with Adam Smith
that they identified wealth — an income —
with money; but they very often expressed
themselves as if they did so, and that also
is of importance. Otherwise their reasoning
is as a rule easy to follow, which does not
mean that it is correct. Believing that consumption in itself was of no value they
came by easy strides to the conclusion that
only an excess of income over expenditure
increased the riches of a country and that
such an excess could consist only in an inflow of precious metals from abroad. Locke
is perhaps more suggestive than any other
writer on that point. From this followed
naturally insistence upon an increased
stock of money even by writers who could
not explain to what use the money should

be put or those who, like Petty, even believed in the possibility of a superabundance of money.

Most mercantilist writers and statesmen, however, insisted in the first place upon the use of money in circulation; this was in harmony with their general eagerness for trade and commerce, movement and exchange. Although the old ideal of cheapness, which was closely allied to that of plenty, held sway for a long time and perhaps never entirely lost its influence, most mercantilists were at heart inflationists. So far their eagerness for increased circulation was a foregone conclusion; for some form of the quantity theory of money was very widely held. One writer, Samuel Fortrey, found a happy expression for this aspect of mercantilism when he said in 1663: "It might be wished, nothing were cheap amongst us but onely money." This view paved the way for the plausible theories of John Law (1705) and for paper money mercantilism generally. That new departure was in strict accordance with the fundamental tenets of the school but unexpected in its results, since under a paper money regime the precious metals would lose their specific importance and much of the theoretical foundation of mercantilist commercial policy disappear. Belief in the benefits of a rapid circulation was strengthened by arguments to the effect that countries with low prices would have to "sell cheap and buy dear." In the hands of Law, who in this as in other respects could fall back upon Locke, this was elaborated into the doctrine that a plentiful supply of money within a country created a favorable rate of exchange. Almost the only writer showing a clear conception of the fact that rapid circulation by increasing prices became an obstacle to exports was Mun; but he did not follow out the conclusions, which would of course have been subversive of the whole body of mercantilist doctrine.

Lastly, mercantilism implied a general view of society, a fact which is often overlooked. This general attitude was closely akin to that of the successors of the mercantilists, the laissez faire philosophers, in almost all other respects their opposites. Both followed the general trend of modern opinion, replacing religious and moral considerations by belief in unalterable laws of social causation — a rationalism often accompanied by a strictly non-moral and non-humanitarian view of social life. The mercantilists were in agreement with laissez faire philosophers not only in basing their reasoning upon natural law; there are many likenesses as well as marked dissimilarities between the views of the two schools as to general social psychology, for example, between Petty and Hobbes on one side and Bentham on the other.

It is especially noticeable that mercantilist statesmen and writers believed in what was called "freedom of trade," or "free trade"; the utterances of Colbert to that effect are innumerable and in most cases quite seriously meant; sometimes it was even said that all interference with economic life should be avoided. How could mercantilists arrive at their practical measures from such premises? Certainly there is much inconsistency to be accounted for, but their fundamental view is quite clear. Unlike the laissez faire economists they did not base their advocacy of free trade and non-interference with economic life on the existence of a preestablished self-operating harmony. What they meant was that interference should aim at changing causes and not effects, that it was useless to punish unavoidable results without removing their causes. As a paradoxical but very typical mercantilist, Bernard Mandeville, wrote in 1714: "Private vices, by the dextrous management of a skilful politician may be turned into public benefits." The contempt of the mercantilists for religion and ethics, their desire to subject individuals to the state, their belief in a somewhat mechanical social causation without belief in a preestablished harmony, made them even more ruthless in their insistence upon setting aside all sorts of time honored customs and human needs and presented a strong contrast to the fundamentally humanitarian attitudes which followed. Moreover in this respect as in most others the ability of mercantilist statesmen to achieve what was required by their programs was very limited; and their attempts at directing economic life without violence remained mostly on paper. In practise they had recourse to almost all the time honored methods of coercion.

Generally it may be said that mercantilism is of greater interest for what it attempted than for what it achieved. It certainly paved the way for its successors, and the discussions which went on throughout the seventeenth and the early eighteenth century eventually bore fruit, although chiefly through the criticisms they called forth. Great change in the society which mercantilist statesmen had taken over from the Middle Ages did not occur; that was reserved for their successors.

Mercantilism—A Defense

JOHN MAYNARD KEYNES

John Maynard Keynes (1883–1946) is the outstanding economist of the twentieth century. After the First World War his *Economic Consequences of the Peace*, a scathing attack on the Versailles peace settlement, established his reputation as a controversialist. His reputation as an economist rests on *The Treatise of Money* (1930) and the *General Theory of Employment, Interest and Money* (1936), in which he argued that full employment was not an automatic condition, outlined a new theory of the rate of interest, and set out the principles underlying the flows of income and expenditure. He played a leading part in the formulation of the Bretton Woods agreement and the establishment of the International Monetary Fund. A many-sided man, he also produced two volumes of literary essays, *Essays in Persuasion* (1931) and *Essays in Biography* (1933).

I

FOR SOME two hundred years both economic theorists and practical men did not doubt that there is a peculiar advantage to a country in a favourable balance of trade, and grave danger in an unfavourable balance, particularly if it results in an efflux of the precious metals. But for the past one hundred years there has been a remarkable divergence of opinion. The majority of statesmen and practical men in most countries, and nearly half of them even in Great Britain, the home of the opposite view, have remained faithful to the ancient doctrine; whereas almost all economic theorists have held that anxiety concerning such matters is absolutely groundless except on a very short view, since the mechanism of foreign trade is self-adjusting and attempts to interfere with it are not only futile, but greatly impoverish those who practise them because they for-

From *The General Theory of Employment, Interest, and Money* by John Maynard Keynes, 332–50. Reprinted by permission of Harcourt, Brace & World, Inc. and of Macmillan and Co., Ltd.

feit the advantages of the international division of labour. It will be convenient, in accordance with tradition, to designate the older opinion as *Mercantilism* and the newer as *Free Trade*, though these terms, since each of them has both a broader and a narrower signification, must be interpreted with reference to the context.

Generally speaking, modern economists have maintained not merely that there is, as a rule, a balance of gain from the international division of labour sufficient to outweigh such advantages as mercantilist practice can fairly claim, but that the mercantilist argument is based, from start to finish, on an intellectual confusion.

Marshall, for example, although his references to Mercantilism are not altogether unsympathetic, had no regard for their central theory as such and does not even mention those elements of truth in their contentions which I shall examine below. In the same way, the theoretical concessions which free-trade economists have been ready to make in contemporary controversies, relating, for example, to the encouragement of infant industries or to the improvement of the terms of trade, are not concerned with the real substance of the mercantilist case. During the fiscal controversy of the first quarter of the present century I do not remember that any concession was ever allowed by economists to the claim that Protection might increase domestic employment. It will be fairest, perhaps, to quote, as an example, what I wrote myself. So lately as 1923, as a faithful pupil of the classical school who did not at that time doubt what he had been taught and entertained on this matter no reserves at all, wrote: "If there is one thing that Protection can *not* do, it is to cure Unemployment. . . . There are some arguments for Protection, based upon its securing possible but improbable advantages, to which there is no simple answer. But the claim to cure Unemployment involves the Protectionist fallacy in its grossest and crudest form." As for earlier mercantilist theory, no intelligible account was avail-

able; and we were brought up to believe that it was little better than nonsense. So absolutely overwhelming and complete has been the domination of the classical school.

II

Let me first state in my own terms what now seems to me to be the element of scientific truth in mercantilist doctrine. We will then compare this with the actual arguments of the mercantilists. It should be understood that the advantages claimed are avowedly national advantages and are unlikely to benefit the world as a whole.

When a country is growing in wealth somewhat rapidly, the further progress of this happy state of affairs is liable to be interrupted, in conditions of *laissez-faire*, by the insufficiency of the inducements to new investment. Given the social and political environment and the national characteristics which determine the propensity to consume, the well-being of a progressive state essentially depends, for the reasons we have already explained, on the sufficiency of such inducements. They may be found either in home investment or in foreign investment (including in the latter the accumulation of the precious metals), which, between them, make up aggregate investment. In conditions in which the quantity of aggregate investment is determined by the profit motive alone, the opportunities for home investment will be governed, in the long run, by the domestic rate of interest; whilst the volume of foreign investment is necessarily determined by the size of the favourable balance of trade. Thus, in a society where there is no question of direct investment under the aegis of public authority, the economic objects, with which it is reasonable for the government to be preoccupied, are the domestic rate of interest and the balance of foreign trade.

Now, if the wage-unit is somewhat stable and not liable to spontaneous changes of significant magnitude (a condition which is almost always satisfied), if the state of liquidity-preference is somewhat stable, taken as an average of its short-period fluctuations, and if banking conventions are also stable, the rate of interest will tend to be governed by the quantity of the precious metals, measured in terms of the wage-unit, available to satisfy the community's deside for liquidity. At the same time, in an age in which substantial foreign loans and the outright ownership of wealth located abroad are scarcely practicable, increases and decreases in the quantity of the precious metals will largely depend on whether the balance of trade is favourable or unfavourable.

Thus, as it happens, a preoccupation on the part of the authorities with a favourable balance of trade served *both* purposes; and was, furthermore, the only available means of promoting them. At a time when the authorities had no direct control over the domestic rate of interest or the other inducements to home investment, measures to increase the favourable balance of trade were the only *direct* means at their disposal for increasing foreign investment; and, at the same time, the effect of a favourable balance of trade on the influx of the precious metals was their only *indirect* means of reducing the domestic rate of interest and so increasing the inducement to home investment.

There are, however, two limitations on the success of this policy which must not be overlooked. If the domestic rate of interest falls so low that the volume of investment is sufficiently stimulated to raise employment to a level which breaks through some of the critical points at which the wage-unit rises, the increase in the domestic level of costs will begin to react unfavourably on the balance of foreign trade, so that the effort to increase the latter will have overreached and defeated itself. Again, if the domestic rate of interest falls so low relatively to rates of interest elsewhere as to stimulate a volume of foreign lending which is disproportionate to the favourable balance, there may ensue an efflux of the precious metals sufficient to reverse the advantages previously obtained. The risk of one or other of these limitations

becoming operative is increased in the case of a country which is large and internationally important by the fact that, in conditions where the current output of the precious metals from the mines is on a relatively small scale, an influx of money into one country means an efflux from another; so that the adverse effects of rising costs and falling rates of interest at home may be accentuated (if the mercantilist policy is pushed too far) by falling costs and rising rates of interest abroad.

The economic history of Spain in the latter part of the fifteenth and in the sixteenth centuries provides an example of a country whose foreign trade was destroyed by the effect on the wage-unit of an excessive abundance of the precious metals. Great Britain in the pre-war years of the twentieth century provides an example of a country in which the excessive facilities for foreign lending and the purchase of properties abroad frequently stood in the way of the decline in the domestic rate of interest which was required to ensure full employment at home. The history of India at all times has provided an example of a country impoverished by a preference for liquidity amounting to so strong a passion that even an enormous and chronic influx of the precious metals has been insufficient to bring down the rate of interest to a level which was compatible with the growth of real wealth.

Nevertheless, if we contemplate a society with a somewhat stable wage-unit, with national characteristics which determine the propensity to consume and the preference for liquidity, and with a monetary system which rigidly links the quantity of money to the stock of the precious metals, it will be essential for the maintenance of prosperity that the authorities should pay close attention to the state of the balance of trade. For a favourable balance, provided it is not too large, will prove extremely stimulating; while an unfavourable balance may soon produce a state of persistent depression.

It does not follow from this that the

maximum degree of restriction of imports will promote the maximum favourable balance of trade. The earlier mercantilists laid great emphasis on this and were often to be found opposing trade restrictions because on a long view they were liable to operate adversely to a favourable balance. It is, indeed, arguable that in the special circumstances of mid-nineteenth-century Great Britain an almost complete freedom of trade was the policy most conducive to the development of a favourable balance. Contemporary experience of trade restrictions in post-war Europe offers manifold examples of ill-conceived impediments on freedom which, designed to improve the favourable balance, had in fact a contrary tendency.

For this and other reasons the reader must not reach a premature conclusion as to the *practical* policy to which our argument leads up. There are strong presumptions of a general character against trade restrictions unless they can be justified on special grounds. The advantages of the international division of labour are real and substantial, even though the classical school greatly overstressed them. The fact that the advantage which our own country gains from a favourable balance is liable to involve an equal disadvantage to some other country (a point to which the mercantilists were fully alive) means not only that great moderation is necessary, so that a country secures for itself no larger a share of the stock of the precious metals than is fair and reasonable, but also that an immoderate policy may lead to a senseless international competition for a favourable balance which injures all alike. And finally, a policy of trade restrictions is a treacherous instrument even for the attainment of its ostensible object, since private interest, administrative incompetence and the intrinsic difficulty of the task may divert it into producing results directly opposite to those intended.

Thus, the weight of my criticism is directed against the inadequacy of the *theoretical* foundations of the *laissez-faire* doctrine upon which I was brought up and which for many years I taught — against the notion that the rate of interest and the volume of investment are self-adjusting at the optimum level, so that preoccupation with the balance of trade is a waste of time. For we, the faculty of economists, prove to have been guilty of presumptuous error in treating as a puerile obsession what for centuries has been a prime object of practical statecraft.

Under the influence of this faulty theory the City of London gradually devised the most dangerous technique for the maintenance of equilibrium which can possibly be imagined, namely, the technique of bank rate coupled with a rigid parity of the foreign exchanges. For this meant that the objective of maintaining a domestic rate of interest consistent with full employment was wholly ruled out. Since, in practice, it is impossible to neglect the balance of payments, a means of controlling it was evolved which, instead of protecting the domestic rate of interest, sacrificed it to the operation of blind forces. Recently, practical bankers in London have learnt much, and one can almost hope that in Great Britain the technique of bank rate will never be used again to protect the foreign balance in conditions in which it is likely to cause unemployment at home.

Regarded as the theory of the individual firm and of the distribution of the product resulting from the employment of a given quantity of resources, the classical theory has made a contribution to economic thinking which cannot be impugned. It is impossible to think clearly on the subject without this theory as a part of one's apparatus of thought. I must not be supposed to question this in calling attention to their neglect of what was valuable in their predecessors. Nevertheless, as a contribution to statecraft, which is concerned with the economic system as whole and with securing the optimum employment of the system's entire resources, the methods of the early pioneers of economic thinking in the sixteenth and seventeenth centuries may have attained to fragments of practical wisdom which the unrealistic abstractions of Ricardo first forgot and then obliterated. There was wisdom in their intense preoccupation with keeping down the rate of interest by means of usury laws (to which we will return later in this chapter), by maintaining the domestic stock of money and by discouraging rises in the wage-unit; and in their readiness in the last resort to restore the stock of money by devaluation, if it had become plainly deficient through an unavoidable foreign drain, a rise in the wage-unit, or any other cause.

III

The early pioneers of economic thinking may have hit upon their maxims of practical wisdom without having had much cognisance of the underlying theoretical grounds. Let us, therefore, examine briefly the reasons they gave as well as what they recommended.

(1) Mercantilist thought never supposed that there was a self-adjusting tendency by which the rate of interest would be established at the appropriate level. On the contrary they were emphatic that an unduly high rate of interest was the main obstacle to the growth of wealth; and they were even aware that the rate of interest depended on liquidity-preference and the quantity of money. They were concerned both with diminishing liquidity-preference and with increasing the quantity of money, and several of them made it clear that their preoccupation with increasing the quantity of money was due to their desire to diminish the rate of interest.

*   *   *

How easily the mercantilist mind distinguished between the rate of interest and the marginal efficiency of capital is illustrated by a passage (printed in 1621) which Locke quotes from *A Letter to a Friend concerning Usury*: "High Interest decays Trade. The advantage from Interest is greater than the Profit from Trade, which makes the rich Merchants give over, and put out their Stock to Interest, and the

lesser Merchants Break." Fortrey (*England's Interest and Improvement*, 1663) affords another example of the stress laid on a low rate of interest as a means of increasing wealth.

The mercantilists did not overlook the point that, if an excessive liquidity-preference were to withdraw the influx of precious metals into hoards, the advantage to the rate of interest would be lost. In some cases (*e.g.* Mun) the object of enhancing the power of the State led them, nevertheless, to advocate the accumulation of state treasure. But others [*e.g.* Schrötter] frankly opposed this policy. . . .

(2) The mercantilists were aware of the fallacy of cheapness and the danger that excessive competition may turn the terms of trade against a country. Thus Malynes wrote in his *Lex Mercatoria* (1622): "Strive not to undersell others to the hurt of the Commonwealth, under colour to increase trade: for trade doth not increase when commodities are good cheap, because the cheapness proceedeth of the small request and scarcity of money, which maketh things cheap: so that the contrary augmeneth trade, when there is plenty of money, and commodities become dearer being in request.". . .

(3) The mercantilists were the originals of "the fear of goods" and the scarcity of money as causes of unemployment which the classicals were to denounce two centuries later as an absurdity. . . .

Mercantilists were conscious that their policy, as Professor Heckscher puts it, "killed two birds with one stone." "On the one hand the country was rid of an unwelcome surplus of goods, which was believed to result in unemployment, while on the other the total stock of money in the country was increased," with the resulting advantages of a fall in the rate of interest.

It is impossible to study the notions to which the mercantilists were led by their actual experiences, without perceiving that there has been a chronic tendency throughout human history for the propensity to save to be stronger than the inducement to invest. The weakness of the inducement to invest has been at all times the key to the economic problem. To-day the explanation of the weakness of this inducement may chiefly lie in the extent of existing accumulations; whereas, formerly, risks and hazards of all kinds may have played a larger part. But the result is the same. The desire of the individual to augment his personal wealth by abstaining from consumption has usually been stronger than the inducement to the entrepreneur to augment the national wealth by employing labour on the construction of durable assets.

(4) The mercantilists were under no illusions as to the nationalistic character of their policies and their tendency to promote war. It was *national* advantage and *relative* strength at which they were admittedly aiming.

We may criticise them for the apparent indifference with which they accepted this inevitable consequence of an international monetary system. But intellectually their realism is much preferable to the confused thinking of contemporary advocates of an international fixed gold standard and *laissez-faire* in international lending, who believe that it is precisely these policies which will best promote peace.

For in an economy subject to money contracts and customs more or less fixed over an appreciable period of time, where the quantity of the domestic circulation and the domestic rate of interest are primarily determined by the balance of payments, as they were in Great Britain before the war, there is no orthodox means open to the authorities for countering unemployment at home except by struggling for an export surplus and an import of the monetary metal at the expense of their neighbours. Never in history was there a method devised of such efficacy for setting each country's advantage at variance with its neighbours' as the international gold (or, formerly, silver) standard. For it made domestic prosperity directly dependent on a competitive pursuit of markets and a competitive appetite for the precious metals. When by happy accident the new supplies of gold and silver were comparatively abundant, the struggle might be somewhat abated. But with the growth of wealth and the diminishing marginal propensity to consume, it has tended to become increasingly internecine. The part played by orthodox economists, whose common sense has been insufficient to check their faulty logic, has been disastrous to the latest act. For when in their blind struggle for an escape, some countries have thrown off the obligations which had previously rendered impossible an autonomous rate of interest, these economists have taught that a restoration of the former shackles is a necessary first step to a general recovery.

In truth the opposite holds good. It is the policy of an autonomous rate of interest, unimpeded by international preoccupations, and of a national investment programme directed to an optimum level of domestic employment which is twice blessed in the sense that it helps ourselves and our neighbours at the same time. And it is the simultaneous pursuit of these policies by all countries together which is capable of restoring economic health and strength internationally, whether we measure it by the level of domestic employment or by the volume of international trade.

IV

The mercantilists perceived the existence of the problem without being able to push their analysis to the point of solving it. But the classical school ignored the problem, as a consequence of introducing into their premises conditions which involved its non-existence; with the result of creating a cleavage between the conclusions of economic theory and those of common sense. The extraordinary achievement of the classical theory was to overcome the beliefs of the "natural man" and, at the same time, to be wrong.

Mercantilism as a System of Public Finance

HERBERT HEATON

Herbert Heaton (born 1890) is an Englishman whose academic career has taken place in the U.S.A. He was a full professor at the University of Minnesota from 1927 until his retirement in 1958. Best known for his *Economic History of Europe,* his more specialist work was concerned with the major industry of his home county, about which he published *The Yorkshire Woollen and Worsted Industries from the Earliest Times up to the Industrial Revolution* (1920). He is a master of clear, concise, and witty exposition, as the following passage, taken from a long review of Heckscher's *Mercantilism,* shows.

To HECKSCHER, as to all other writers on the subject, mercantilism is not a compact, consistent *ism.* Rather it is "only an instrumental concept which, if aptly chosen, should enable us to understand a particular historical period more clearly than we otherwise might" (I, 19). Its content is that "phase in the history of economic policy" which lies between the end of the Middle Ages and the dawn of the age of laissez faire. The chronological boundaries vary from country to country, but the sixteenth to eighteenth centuries see the policy in its heyday. During that period mercantilism was the normal approach to "a common European problem" (I, 13). France and England provide the best examples and occupy most of the pages, but similar policies were pursued (and are briefly considered) in Scandinavia, the German states, Italy, and Spain. Then, as later, statesmen were copycats and imitated each other either in flattery or retaliation.

Only one important country stood outside the mutual-admiration circle. The Netherlands were "less affected by mercantilist tendencies than most other countries"; "they did not really follow mercantilist practice"; and their development was "an antithesis of mercantilism" (I, 351, 352, 353). Yet Dutch policy is neglected except at one point — company organization. Why? What made Holland an exception to the "common European problem"? An examination of the reasons for the Dutch neglect or rejection of mercantilism would have supplied a good "control," a standard for comparison, and an insight into non-mercantilist thinking about economic affairs. One would gladly surrender a hundred pages explaining how or why France or England did things for twenty explaining why the Dutch did not do them.

When Adam Smith reviewed and reviled "the mercantile system," he dealt chiefly with its monetary attitude and its protectionist policy. When Schmoller wrote about *The Mercantile System and Its Historical Significance* in 1884, he declared its "innermost kernel is nothing but state-making . . . the total transformation of society and its organization, as well as of the state and its institutions, in the replacing of a local and territorial economic policy by that of the state." To Schmoller's English contemporary, Cunningham, mercantilism was a "system of power," a policy pursued "so that the power of England relatively to other nations might be promoted."

From Herbert Heaton, "Heckscher on Mercantilism," *Journal of Political Economy,* XLV (1937), 370–93. By permission of the author and the editors of the *Journal of Political Economy.*

These three writers thus examined four different aspects — money, protection, unification, and power — but each concentrated on one or two items which seemed important to him. Heckscher embraces all four and adds a fifth, for through the welter of discussion and the smoke of controversy he is able to perceive the emergence of a "fairly uniform conception of general social phenomena in the field of economics" and a "mercantilist conception of society."

Of the five aspects, "Mercantilism as a Unifying System" occupies the whole of the first volume and more than half of the total text. The theme can be stated fairly simply. The mercantilist state found itself confronted with two legacies of medieval particularism, in the form of more or less independent feudal lords on the one hand, and more or less autonomous towns on the other. The lords levied tolls, sometimes operated a mint, had their own systems of weights and measures, and so forth; the result was confusion worse confounded, and heavy financial burdens on goods that had to be moved any great distance. The towns sought to pursue a selfish economic policy, trying to monopolize the economic life of the surrounding countryside, to exploit foreigners passing through the town, to control industry and trade by the guild system, and to foster their citizens' external trade.

When a territorial state gained control of lord and town, it sought to add economic unity to political. It tried to remove, lighten, or simplify the tolls and customs, to get uniformity of weights and measures, and to dispel the currency chaos by making a royal monopoly of minting. It took charge of the regulation of industry, either by bringing the guilds under its complete control, and then extending their scope, or by passing laws dealing with producers and products. It took charge of foreign trade by granting charters to regulated or joint-stock companies, thus conferring on them a monopoly of the trade with certain regions and giving them sovereign political power in distant continents.

The story of these efforts in England, France, and Germany is told at great length. . . .

Yet I doubt whether Heckscher is justified in subjecting us to 423 pages on the theme of "Mercantilism as a Unifying System," for the very simple reason that very little unifying — or even uniformifying — was accomplished. One grows weary of reading a long account of this or that effort and then reaching some such phrase as "confusion reigned supreme," "little was accomplished," "the work of unification was insignificant," and so on. Three successes of some importance are chronicled: (1) the Statute of Artificers (1563), which dealt with wages regulation, apprenticeship, etc., in England; (2) Colbert's tariff of 1664, which consolidated export and import duties, abolished many tolls, and substituted uniform rates in the "five great farms" (tax farm areas), which covered about three-eighths of France; and (3) some unification of customs administration in seventeenth-century Sweden. But two of these three achievements were in countries (Sweden and England) that were not seriously disintegrated and stood in little need of unification; so we are left with Colbert's one big success, a handful of questionable minor successes, and a host of failures, of which Colbert's foreign-trade companies may be mentioned as examples. Hence mercantilism's first aspect might well be called "Love's Labour's Lost," "Much Ado about Nothing," or "Original Sin versus Political Futility."

Faced with these facts, and pricked by the remark of a German critic that economic unity was not an important mercantilist aim, Heckscher has retreated somewhat. In his "revision" he admits:

It is not only that the attempts at unity were, with few exceptions, failures — such was the result of the majority of mercantilist measures; even these attempts themselves were to a great extent half-hearted. It is difficult to find more than two bold attempts in this direction in the leading countries. . . . This consideration gives rise to a suspicion that mercantilist statesmen did not take their unifying work seriously [*Econ. Hist. Rev.*, p. 46].

But he does insist that "they were, however, unable to shirk altogether the task of adapting the medieval framework of European society to new economic and social conditions." It is worth while, therefore, lingering for a moment on Volume I, to ask why so little was accomplished.

Some of the failures lie at the door of defective administration. No one worked harder than Colbert to erect a comprehensive well-organized civil service; yet all his work on toll reform was "undermined by that inveterate cancer of all customs administration of early times, the disobedience and dishonesty of the officials" (I, 105), and much of his industrial regulation suffered the same fate. England did not create an *ad hoc* bureaucracy to supervise the enforcement of her industrial legislation, as Colbert did. Instead she piled much of the work on the overburdened shoulders of the local justices of the peace. Fatigue, indifference, carelessness, or definite defiance of a disliked decree made the justices' work patchy in execution; and when paid officers (searchers) were appointed to enforce laws dealing with cloth, it became necessary to appoint inspectors to watch the searchers, and then supervisors to watch the inspectors. The inefficiency or corruptibility of underpaid customs officers and anti-smuggling squads was notorious.

Some state efforts failed because they could not overcome the strength of local interests vested in and supported by the old order. But probably the chief reason for half-hearted effort or scant success lay in another direction, to which Heckscher has attached inadequate or only incidental importance. Mercantilism had *six* aspects, not five; the sixth was public (or royal) finance, and one might with great cogency maintain it was the most important of the lot. George Unwin may have been wrong when, in Tawney's words, he regarded mercantilism as "a negative and restrictive factor, which

had its principal source, not in any deliberate plan of promoting economic progress, but in the fiscal exigencies of short-sighted and impecunious governments"; but his error was only one of exaggeration, for rarely in framing policy did a government have the deplorable condition of its exchequer far out of mind, and every "projector" who presented a scheme to his ruler stressed the benefit that would directly or indirectly flow into the royal coffers.

If mercantilism was state-building, a picture of the character of the state and of the builder would seem to be a necessary frontispiece or preface. Yet we have to work through to pages 78, 124, and even 178 befort we get a real glimpse of the financial problems which beset and bedeviled mercantilist statesmen. By patching the financial fragments together and adding to them what we know from other sources, we see a state which, in Hauser's words, had the obligations of a modern centralized state but the revenue system of a feudal one. The obligations were heavier because of the greater luxury of the courts, the higher price-level, and the growing cost of wars fought with the new equipment by larger mercenary armies. From 1500 to 1815 war was almost a normal relationship between European states; there were only seven calendar years of peace in the seventeenth century, and Great Britain was at war with someone during 84 of the 165 years between 1650 and 1815. This chronic belligerency affected policies, both political and economic; it also affected pockets and led rulers to wild scrambles for cash wherever they could see any. The royal repudiations, from those of Philip II of Spain to those of Charles II of England, are merely instances where perpetually strained finances snapped. French officials, says Heckscher, were always "bent on collecting enough to cover their expenditure of the next twenty-four hours"; instead of planning reforms which might have been more productive in the long run, "the old method of snatching at whatever lay to hand was followed" (I, 124). The English experience was little less desperate, as Professor Dietz has shown. Elizabeth's parsimony, forced loans, increased rents for crown lands, and other devices failed to make ends meet; and the treasury was running into debt at the rate of £100,000 a year during the last part of her reign. The first two Stuarts struggled equally hard, tried to tap new sources of revenue, and turned old faucets on full; but their extravagance and the Scottish troubles made deficits unavoidable.

In such circumstances, far-reaching schemes for unification or regulation had little chance of being seriously developed if they threatened to check for a moment the flow of revenue. More important still, many plans which, on the surface, seemed to aim at unification, regulation, or the promotion of some industry or trade had a fiscal motive. Let us look at one or two instances. The German princes may have thought reform of tolls desirable, but they did nothing because they "found the internal tolls an indispensable source of income" (I, 78). They needed the money so badly that all considerations of economic unity or search for less obstructive sources of income had to be dismissed. France was not in a much better position, and we are not surprised that after Colbert's new deal of 1664 scarcely anything was accomplished until the Revolution made a clean sweep. But we are surprised to learn the importance of fiscal considerations in the elaborate system of Colbertian industrial regulation. That system has always seemed to be the high-water mark in state efforts to induce or enforce industrial morality, to stamp out "tricks of the trade," to suppress dishonest or defective workmanship, and to oblige craftsmen to produce good articles, especially for the export market. It sought to achieve this end by what might be called a "national guild system"; all producers must be guildsmen, subject to *règlements* issued by the state, and supervised by guild or state inspectors. But having led us,

through 42 pages of description and discussion, to believe that quality through regulated guild monopoly was the mercantilist aim, Heckscher announces that

the foregoing account omits one of the most important features of economic policy, if not the most important of all — namely what is called in French *fiscalisme*. . . . The state, by its intervention, wanted to create large sources of revenue for itself, under the more or less false pretence of guiding industry along the right lines. . . . The state exploited for its own ends the monopolistic advantages which the guilds had secured for their members or the owners of private privileges had secured for themselves [I, 178].

The whole series of industrial regulations "unblushingly served fiscal ends"; their "true purpose was really fiscal." The guild masterships, wardenships, inspectorships, etc., belonged to that vast army of posts, offices, or classes that "were created simply in order that they might be sold" in order to enable "the most powerful European state to carry on from day to day for a number of centuries" (I, 180). "Industrial control thus stood revealed as naked fiscalism," as "a kind of indirect taxation, taxing the consumers through the monopolistic artisans" (I, 181).

England gives fewer instances of fiscalism, but has some. For a time, in late Elizabethan and early Stuart times, favorites at court were given, or allowed to buy, a monopolistic right to supervise a trade, to conduct it, and to pocket (or to share with the crown) the fines, fees, and profits; but this excursion into low finance was quickly checked by the courts or by Parliament, and soon came to a dishonored end. The state attitude toward companies, whether regulated or joint stock, had at least one eye on direct fiscal benefits. The crown frequently regarded the companies as milch kine; it would blithely establish a rival company and violate an old charter if more money could thereby be obtained; it would claim a share of the capital and profit, and lean on the East India Company, the South Sea Company, and, of course, the Bank of England after 1694, for loans. When in the eighteenth century the state found other ways of financing itself, the sale of monopolies to corporations ceased. In view of such evidence, one may ask again why mercantilism as a system of public finance should not be regarded as being vastly more important than considerations of unification.

The Idea of a Mercantile State

ARTHUR VALENTINE JUDGES

Arthur Valentine Judges (born 1898) taught economic history at the London School of Economics until 1948, when he became professor of the history of education at King's College, University of London. As an economic historian his main interest was in the history of early modern Britain. He wrote on the beginnings of banking and edited The Elizabethan Underworld, a collection of tracts. This article is an incisive statement of the sceptical point of view.

VARIOUS MEANINGS have been given to the words *mercantile system* and also to the more austere *mercantilism* which German scholarship has coined for us to use when we wish to attempt a distillation of the policies attributed to practitioners of that system. Most of us would doubtless be ready to admit that these terms of art of the economist have been useful in bringing large groups of facts and theories into focus; and therein lies their justification. But the concepts which they awkwardly try to express have had a steadily diminishing utility in recent years as our knowledge has advanced, and (like other premature generalisations in the history of ideas) it would seem that they are being perpetuated because we shrink from generalising anew.

One of the first things we require of a system is that it should be capable of systematic demonstration; whilst an "ism" to be worthy of serious consideration must offer a coherent doctrine, or at least a handful of settled principles. In what measure can the mercantile system and mercantilism bear scrutiny when we approach them in this fashion?

The truth seems to be that there was never a living doctrine at all, nothing that can be compared with vital philosophies of action like physiocracy or liberalism or Marxism. Mercantilism never had a creed; nor was there a priesthood dedicated to its service. Whilst some of the beliefs which its supposed philosophy is said to have subsumed were still widely and indeed vigorously upheld when the subject was first discovered to have independent reality, no one appears to have offered to defend its essentials or come forward to die fighting for the altar of the faith. The altar was really an affair of archaeological reconstruction. First erected by men who fortified their attachments to their own faith by abusing the discredited and superstitious antics of their ancestors, it was later re-

From A. V. Judges, "The Idea of a Mercantile State," *Transactions of the Royal Historical Society,* fourth series, XXI (1939), 41–69. By permission of the author and the Royal Historical Society.

fashioned with many curious devices by the pious hands of those who wished to persuade themselves that current ideals could be sanctioned by the genius and wisdom of the past.

The discovery of the existence of a body of mercantile beliefs was made in the eighteenth century by men who found security for their own faith in a system of natural law. The bond of mutual sympathy among these observers was created far less by any similarity in their practical recommendations than by their common distrust of the current expedients of statecraft in Western Europe; expedients which seemed designed with an almost cunning premeditation to hinder the maximisation of both happiness and productive capacity by setting up barriers to the economic self-expression of the individual citizen. Quesnay and his disciples the *économistes* in France and Smith in Britain were themselves creators of politico-economic theories claiming universal validity. It was perhaps only natural that they should seek to strengthen the outlines of their own proposals by systematising the theories which they discerned lurking behind the institution that came under their fire. The dummy dragon they set up, articulated and endowed with organic functions by its indignant creators, had the fire of life breathed into it by the avenging angels themselves.

Our earliest introduction to the operative words is in 1763, in the *Philosophie Rurale* of Victor Riquetti, Marquis de Mirabeau, Quesnay's most excitable follower. "Absurd inconsistency of the mercantile system" (*système mercantile*), he writes in a marginal note. The passage is an attack on the idea that a nation profits from the importation of money; and on the same page he ridicules the approximation of the commercial policy of great empires to the standards of a counting-house in words that sound strikingly like a prophetic echo of Adam Smith's well-known invective upon "the sneaking arts of underling tradesmen." Smith was admittedly not unfamiliar with the *Philosophie Rurale*. Is this where he

found the mercantile system patterned in the fashion he himself was to adopt? . . .

The reason for his decision to devote the longest section of the *Wealth of Nations* to an examination of the mercantile system was that he saw it as a system in being — a reality of the contemporary world — which could be documented and assailed by reference to legislation and practice.

When the attack is opened at the beginning of Book IV, the mercantile system seems to have for Smith a fundamental unity of principle. What was this principle? It was not, to be sure, that wealth consists solely in money, or in gold and silver, although this is "a popular notion" introduced to us in the first paragraph, a catch-phrase which even the best English writers had carelessly slipped into accepting in the course of debate. Much of the subsequent discussion has unfortunately been led up a false path by the failure of commentators to observe that the appearance of the mercantile system is delayed until the sixth paragraph of the chapter in question. Here it is announced as the reasoning of the merchants who in the seventeenth century rebelled against the attempts of government to prohibit the international traffic in bullion. Their libertarian arguments brought conviction to the authorities, at least in some countries, and the consequence was a lifting of restraints laid upon the export of gold and silver. To create conviction it was, however, necessary to appeal to current prejudices. Thomas Mun and the other tractarians of the commercial school accordingly justified their plea for the extension of foreign trade (for which they had their proper motives) by showing that, suitably managed, commerce with other nations enriched the country. The scientific study of the bases of national prosperity was not of course a matter upon which they had a specialist's claim to offer opinion, but, as they were in possession of the platform, it was not unnatural that merchants should claim that they were the principal benefactors. *England's Treasure by Forraign Trade*, the title of Mun's second and posthumous contribution to political economy, published in 1664, could be accepted as the slogan of this school of commercial expansion. Out of this literature arose the calculus of the balance of trade, a touchstone of principle which was to determine what forms of exchange might be encouraged as tending to yield a net balance in treasure and what forms should be discouraged on account of the drain of precious metal they set in motion.

Smith was not greatly concerned, I believe, to discover whether or not the equation *money equals wealth* — the popular maxim to which most of his predecessors had paid occasional lip-service — was a vital ingredient in the "system." It is rather the consequences of the deplorable behaviour of legislators clumsily trying to execute the injunctions of the balance theorists by means of tariffs, prohibitions, drawbacks, bounties and commercial monopolies, that provokes him to the fullest use of his analytical skill and deflating satire. Except in his reflections on the marketing of corn, he is careful to exclude by implication a large range of internal restrictions from the operations of mercantile statecraft. But in almost every field he saw very clearly that public interference was wasteful and corrupt, prodigal above all of administrative effort. This helps to explain his exaggeration of the malignancy and power of gild control in the corporate towns and his distrust of joint-stock enterprise with its tradition of privilege and licensed incompetence. The conclusions which he had previously reached in his Edinburgh lectures by a process of *a priori* reasoning starting from the principle of Natural Liberty, he now re-established with a great wealth of inductive argument supported by wide historical reading and empirical experience of the problems of administration. The effect was overwhelming.

As with the economic writings of Bentham, we are left with a picture of the waste and inefficiency of most forms of public interference as then practised, but not with the sense that the State direction of human affairs is by definition nugatory. Indeed, whoever attempts the instructive task of culling from the works of Adam Smith a list of what Bentham would call the proper *agenda* of public authority must be surprised by the amplitude of his reservations to any thorough-going notion of a *laissez-faire* policy, even within the field of overseas trade.

For many years the study of economic thought as an historical phenomenon was allowed to drop.

*   *   *

Malthus, Ricardo, James Mill and Torrens have no constructive analysis to offer of pre-Smithian thought and policy. But Nassau Senior in his Oxford lectures in 1827 devoted part of his time to an examination of the mercantile system, "which at present clogs all our actions and disturbs all our reasonings." He discussed its monetary aspects at some length in tones of shocked disapproval, summed up the commercial restrictions as having been contrived to produce individual gain at the cost of the common loss, remarking that public opinion noticed only the concentration of gain and seemed unaware of the diffusion of the loss. Unless I am mistaken, this was the first broadside assault on the "system" since the *Wealth of Nations,* and it is important for our purpose because Senior passed from the balance-of-trade policies to some reflections on national jealousies and the manifest aim of mercantile policy to be independent of foreign commodities. This leads to the destruction of the mutul security of nations, to say nothing of privation at home. "The half-naked subjects of Caractacus were doubtless independent of foreign supplies, and so is the semi-barbarian who burrows in the ruins of Persepolis, and gathers his dates among the ruins of palaces."

Autarchy, or self-sufficiency for purposes of defence, had now been brought in to widen the supposed objects of mercantile policy.

*   *   *

The English economists, who never went far beyond the conception for which Adam Smith takes credit as chief inventor, viewed the mercantile system as an agglomeration of commercial interferences fortified by a monetary fallacy which was itself based upon a misunderstanding of the real nature of international exchange. The approach was highly unsympathetic, the treatment limited as to period and range. It was not until Bagehot and Cliffe Leslie protested against the claims of universality which had been advanced for the abstract political economy of a highly capitalised and competitive society that English thought became infected with the idea that "unorthodox" policies might have been living necessities for economic communities in their backward days. Cliffe Leslie even suggested that the classical definitions of wealth — mere abstractions as they looked to him — originated in opposition to the doctrines "erroneously imputed to the mercantile School," and were no more than negative statements.

Germany was the proper nursery of the generalised view of the mercantile state.

* * *

Fichte, the spiritual father of the modern totalitarian state, had reacted against the internationalism of Smith, and desired to safeguard the rule of natural law within a fenced-in territorial enclosure closed against the marauding incursions of flag-waving bagmen. But the full revolt against Manchester liberalism was delayed until List had made out his — journalistically effective — case for the tariff protection of industrial economies in an immature stage of development, and until Roscher and Knies had demonstrated the necessity for studying economic concepts and rules of action as products of the time and circumstances wherein they arose. Economics in the hands of their followers was no abstract science, but the study of the laws of evolution stage by stage as exhibited in the life of nations. It has sometimes been said that members of the school were not economists at all, but

historians or sociologists; and there is just enough truth in this to explain Menger's complaint that "the historians have stepped upon the territory of our science like foreign conquerors, in order to force upon us their language and their customs, their terminology and their methods." Intolerance, not to say malignity, was displayed on both sides when the great struggle opened in the seventies between the respective supporters of the inductive and deductive methods. The younger historical school was forced into an untenable position. Little of what it endeavoured to contribute to economic theory has stood the test of time; but its services to history have had more enduring value, if only for its examination of the springs of political action.

The mercantile state naturally received close attention. In this atmosphere the proper course was not to explode its reputed fallacies but to explain its reality as a stage in the growth of society. Features of bygone economic policy which would have been dismissed elsewhere as irrelevant to the discussion were investigated with loving care as examples of paternalist mercantile strategy. For Roscher a system which had lasted for centuries could not be wholly erroneous, and was worthy of examination. It struck him, for example, that an immensely significant feature of benevolent despotism, and of early economic discussion generally, was the insistence, whether for agricultural, industrial or military reasons, on adequate measures for encouraging population growth. Hildebrand and Bücher developed, though in different fashion, the idea of stages in economic progress from the primitive to the complex. In the latter's judgment the State was compelled by historical necessity to employ measures of guidance in nursing the community through the critical transition from town economy to national economy, until liberalism could at length be given rein for *its* formative career. Not infrequently the state, in the drive towards the goal, manipulated its material into forms unduly artificial. But "the theory of the balance of trade became a necessity when the transition [towards a commercial economy] indispensably postulated the increase of the monetary medium of circulation." Professor Sombart has more recently followed up this idea, using a different framework of stages, in this treatment of mercantilism as the political economy of early capitalism.

It was left for Gustav Schmoller to create a synthetic picture of mercantilism in rounding off the work of his predecessors. This he accomplished using a remarkably deep intuition of the forces underlying public policy in combination with a strong sense of the transcendence of the human will in a world where systematic laws of economic life were only valid on a superficial reckoning. It is hardly an exaggeration to say that he formed his notion of mercantile policy on the study of the struggle for unification and national self-expression guided by the electors and kings of Prussia. As a process of State-building it was concerned as much to provide for the fluidity of resources and products within the country by the removal of tolls, local privileges and currency defects, as to compel the respect of the country's neighbours by a spirited economic policy along and beyond the frontiers. It advocated free-trade or prohibition principles according to the circumstances of the case; and not only according to concrete conditions, but according to the goal towards which the country was striving. The state was a formative agent; it gave existence to organised society; and both political and economic life were forces to be regulated by the government. "The mercantilist ideal was not only the legitimate ideal for those centuries but the only proper end. And the ends aimed at have not yet completely lost their legitimacy," he wrote in 1900. Only a firm and enlightened central authority could coordinate the necessary measures for the creation of a national economy (*Volkswirtschaft*) out of anarchy. Such a conviction led him to the somewhat startling conclusion that the economic decline of the Netherlands was caused by the exclusion from

public life of the House of Orange in the Stadtholderless period, 1650–72.

Much proceeds from Schmoller's prime assumption that state agencies were more effective in pushing trade and capturing fields of enterprise than the unhampered activity of private traders could have been. But it is idle to seek to discover from the wealth of apparently conflicting examples offered in his writings whether mercantilism favoured the use of economic means to serve the ends of national greatness, or the use of political means to achieve successes in the industrial and commercial spheres. There is no fundamental distinction to be drawn between the kinds of means employed by the purposeful and ruthless state authority. The Western powers traded with their rivals while at war with them, and fought them with prohibitions and Navigation Acts while nominally at peace.

The heroic struggle of the Dutch for religious freedom . . . displays itself . . . as a century-long war for the conquest of the East Indian colonies, and the equally long privateering assault on the silver fleets of Spain and the Spanish-American colonial trade. . . . Even the expedition of Gustavus Adolphus to Germany was a move in the game which was being played for the trade of the Baltic.

Schmoller's range of illustration seems to permit no aspect of state activity within a span of centuries to escape the comprehensiveness of his definition. Even the balance-of-trade policies have their place, although "the whole idea and doctrine of the balance of trade . . . was only the secondary consequence of a conception of economic processes which grouped them according to States."

In 1868 at the age of nineteen William Cunningham went to continue his university studies in Germany. That he chose to go to Tübingen, Schmoller's old university, is no more than a coincidence. That he came home profoundly influenced by German conceptions of the state and German notions of order and discipline is a fact which has a bearing on his intellectual progress. Fourteen years later *The Growth of English Industry and Commerce* made its first and, one might say, embryonic appearance, in a single volume. The progress of this remarkable book through its successive editions is in a very real sense a measure of the advance of economic history in England in Cunningham's working lifetime. It was obvious from the beginning that the title was a misnomer. The book was a study of the rise of authoritarianism and its decline, and "the fruitfulness . . . of this field of study . . . had to be demonstrated," as Professor Scott has pointed out, "in the face of the traditions of the Classical School." When the 1892 edition appeared it was made the object of a vigorous attack by W. A. S. Hewins, who was in a few years to become the first Director of the London School of Economics. Hewins was shocked by Cunningham's indiscriminate praise for regulative measures. To call the Corn Bounty Act of 1689 "a masterly stroke of policy" which proved itself to be the corner-stone of English prosperity in the eighteenth century, was, he thought, not so much excessive as wrong-headed. For Cunningham, he suggested, the *pursuit of national power* performed the same functions as prime mover in the seventeenth century as *desire of wealth* did in the nineteenth. He paraphrased Cunningham unkindly but not untruly in a *pastiche* which must have stung his victim:

The mercantile system is concerned with man only as a being who pursues national power, and who is capable of judging of the comparative efficacy of means to that end. It makes entire abstraction of every other human passion or motive, except those which may be regarded as perpetually antagonising principles to the pursuit of national power — viz., neglect of shipping and aversion to a fish diet.

Cunningham's rejoinder was not very effective; but he stuck to his belief in the Corn Bounty Act and the fish diet. Already he was interested in projects for the reconstruction of commercial policy. The South African War and Chamberlain's Tariff Reform proposals swept him on to the public platform, as they swept Hewins himself into the Tariff Commission, as an advocate of imperial preference. The third edition of the *Modern Times* section of the History appeared in 1903 with a startling epilogue. *Laissez-faire* had been a manifest failure. How could a directed national policy repair the damage? The postscript was in reality a protectionist tract, tricked out with historical parallels. Bismarck's socialism from above, for instance, is seen to bear a curious resemblance to the work of the early Stuart Council. The tone of this polemic was modified in subsequent editions; but Cunningham's affection for the alleged mercantilist policy of Burleigh — who "was wonderfully successful in reducing the waste which had come to be so generally current in the fifteenth century" — his belief that the essential policy of common or "general interest" in the old Colonial System was right, even his suspicion that the genuine spirit of regulative control had been thwarted by the growth of democratic institutions during the period which he oddly described as the era of Parliamentary Colbertism — these convictions remained until the end.

Cunningham had indeed developed the generalised view of mercantilism in a more convincing fashion than had any other writer or teacher. His was perhaps a more satisfying exposition than the German attempts because it was inspired in the main by the institutional life-story of a single well-knit community. English examples of the operation of the unifying principles came too early, or were too limited, to distract attention seriously from the great topics of naval efficiency and imperial solidarity which run as coloured threads through his examination of the growth of national policy; yet industrial and social control receive adequate attention as expressions of mercantile trends.

The influence of this great teacher has been such that students of history have experienced no little difficulty in preserving appreciation for whatever may be the merits of the restricted view. Sir William Ashley was more cautious than Cunningham, but he was under the spell of *Historismus* with its love of stages and time sequences. Even the title of his most important historical work, *An Introduction to English Economic History and Theory,* displays a challenge. George Unwin, who took a different side in the South African War controversy, brought a mind of tougher fibre than Cunningham's to bear on the history of paternalist regulation, and found it wanting in sincerity and effectiveness. He emphasised "the tendency to over-estimate the active part which wise forethought and the deliberate pursuit of clear ideas has played in the economic history of nations," at the same time admitting that positive interference measures had shaped the course of events in a very definite and sometimes disastrous fashion. "It is an undoubted fact, says Voltaire somewhere, that spells and incantations are capable of destroying whole flocks of sheep, if accompanied by sufficient quantities of arsenic." This saying had always appeared to Unwin "to afford a suggestive introduction to the study of the influence of ideas, of theory, upon economic development." We may approve or disapprove of his scepticism; we may hold that he even exaggerated the influence of thought upon policy; it can hardly be conceded that he gave sharper definition to the idea of the mercantile state.

The responsibility for questioning the propriety of the generalised description has been lightly assumed by one or two economists in this country and America; but our monographs and textbooks in economic history are still vaguely comprehensive in their use of terms; and it may be that the reluctance of writers to overhaul their terminological equipment has been to some extent justified by certain considerations arising out of the fuller examination of pre-Smithian economic writings which has been in progress during the last few years. Professor Heckscher of Stockholm, in what will doubtless establish itself as the classic exposition of the thought and policy of the period of early capitalism in Europe, has produced an eclectic survey of the manifold tendencies of that age. His masterly analysis of conflicting trends brings out certain common assumptions which may have caused statesmen to close their eyes to the often fundamental divergence of interest existing among consumers, producers and distributing agencies, so that they allowed themselves to be dominated now by "love of goods," now by "fear of goods"; now by the glamour of bullion, now by the magical appeal of paper-money inflation. But when all has been said I think the highest common factor in the harvest of notions and policies brought to the surface by Professor Heckscher's efficient trawl can be no more than this: a belief in official intervention as a corrective to evils which must arise from the neglect of public interest in the actions of individuals and of institutions subordinate to the political authority. And the political authority wanted unity and wanted power; not, surely, exceptional ends in the history of human programmes!

It is proper, however, to insist on the book's positive contributions to the study of the subject. Only one can be mentioned here. In demonstrating that the theory of money looked upon currency from two points of view Professor Heckscher has cleared the field for a more systematic approach. It was no longer necessary to elevate bullion to a special position as a store of value, and to some extent as a factor of production, when credit instruments and bank money began to show their ability to function in place of gold and silver. The balance-of-trade concepts of Misselden and Serra were no longer deadly instruments in eighteenth-century controversy. But the consideration of circulating money, money as a means of exchange and as a price-determinant, whatever might be its material composition, was almost as lively an issue as it came to be later on in the bullion debates. The control of the rate of interest and the lowering of the price of labour were now the practical questions. Such things did prompt theoretical analysis. On the one hand rising prices signified the ability to clear stocks, increase sales, raise rents; on the other, the reduction of the cost of productive agents, especially labour, would allow the country to force manufactured goods on its neighbours. Under suitable control conditions a favourable trading balance was ardently to be desired because it might be held to indicate the sending out of embodied labour effort — an artificial and, so to speak, gratuitous product — in exchange for the indestructible material on which the circulating media could be still further expanded — or often just for the satisfaction of keeping people at work. The full employment of labour was desired for many reasons. It is worth recalling, for example, that from the end of Elizabeth's reign the cost of poor relief in this country fell on the ratepayers. And a careful examination of the arguments relating to production for export used in Great Britain from the Restoration onwards has suggested to more than one investigator — I have in mind Professor Viner of Chicago and Dr. E. A. J. Johnson of Cornell in particular — a new variant of the restricted view of mercantilism; the balance of trade being conceived in terms, not of gold and silver, but of the number of labourers, or units of labour, applied to the commodities exchanged in international trade. The policy, of course, aimed at an *excess* of such exports of realised labour.

So we have to add to our accumulated stock a fresh body of interpretation — an important and acceptable increment, it is true; but is the subject of our discussion not becoming somewhat embarrassingly miscellaneous? Are we prepared to allow that every act of authority involving interference displayed some element of the true tradition of the mercantilist spirit? There are indications that at any moment we may be confronted with an attempt to resurrect and pin down in a display cabinet the mercantilist theory of the disposition of capital resources at home and abroad. How, if I may pose one conundrum, ought one to regard the Bubble Act of 1720? Was this a mercantilist measure? It threatened with all the penalties of praemunire the promoters of any association of investors which had shares offered for public subscription, unless, that is, a charter could be produced. It was restrictive, certainly; paternalist in its intention to protect the ignorant investor; and it may be held to have interfered seriously with the free employment of the accumulated capital of several generations. But might it not be treated as an anti-mercantilist gesture? It foreshadowed the ultimate doom of the great licensed monopolies. Was it not, moreover, a vindication of the principle of private enterprise? "Trade seldom requires the aid of such combinations," roundly asserted the Attorney-General in 1761, "but thrives better when left open to the free speculations of private men." How does the Act work into Adam Smith's treatment of corporations? What would Schmoller have made of it? Finally, what do its consequences mean when treated as far as possible on their own merits — divorced from early Stuart patent procedure on the one hand, and the principles of nineteenth-century company law on the other?

Any programme of limited investigation into the phenomena of policy must proceed by employing the well-known methods of inductive inquiry until the material is isolated and built into some sort of pattern. At every stage the testing and application of general ideas must, of course, go on, whether the interpretation deals with the monetary, or the labour, or the capital, or the land, or the governmental, or any other aspect of policy. Must the idea, or rather complex of ideas, of the mercantile state necessarily be forced into the process until it dominates the whole structure of the finished work? In this respect, at least, the critics among the economists of current historical method seem to be mistaken. We ought perhaps to set out with a better equipment of theoretical concepts; but there is one little group of postulates we could well dispense with.

The plea I wish to advance is that we

should now consider ourselves absolved from the necessity of having to reconcile the conclusions derived from detailed researches into the antecedents and effects of edicts, statutes and municipal by-laws, spread over the whole European and colonial field within a period of more than three centuries, with the canons of an imaginary system conceived by economists for purposes of theoretical exposition and mishandled by historians in the service of their political ideals. If I have interpreted aright the doctrinal syntheses to which numberless historians have tried to accommodate themselves, it is clear that many of the rationalised ambitions and fears and jealousies which are their subject matter have been active throughout the world, as perhaps never before, since the economic crisis of 1931. It might be argued to the disadvantage of the present day that what we have gained in logical precision we have lost in sincerity; for it has never been suggested that the restrictionists of the old school claimed for the measures they proposed in their own country's favour that they brought great benefits to other communities.

In the history of nations the brief episode of economic individualism, reflecting, as Continental observers have never tired of reminding us, the special conditions and requirements of this country, may prove to have been a unique experience. The word *neo-mercantilism* is already appearing with ominous frequency in serious discussions. Are we threatened with a further extension of the old aspects and stages? There appears to be much to be said for over-hauling our armoury of classes and categories in order that we may avail ourselves of instruments of greater precision. It would be false to the spirit of a paper which has been almost entirely destructive in intention to suggest even a provisional inventory of more suitable equipment. Moreover, "finding flaws in labels is much easier than finding patently superior substitutes."

I can only suggest that such simple expressions as *national policy* would have more meaning if they could be applied without inward misgivings to all and every chapter in the history of a nation; for even a *laissez-faire* State has an economic policy, and may be striving for greatness.

Power versus Plenty

JACOB VINER

Jacob Viner (born 1892) was born in Montreal and was educated at Mc-
Gill and Harvard universities. Professor of economics at Princeton from 1946
to 1960, his best-known work is his *Studies in the Theory of International Trade*,
but he has many other books and articles, notably in the field of international
trade and economic development, to his credit. He has been active also in
public life. In this article he makes a telling criticism of Heckscher's view of
mercantilism.

WHAT is the correct interpretation of mercantilist doctrine and practice with respect to the roles of power and plenty as ends of national policy? I believe that practically all mercantilists, whatever the period, country, or status of the particular individual, would have subscribed to all of the following propositions: (1) wealth is an absolutely essential means to power, whether for security or for aggression; (2) power is essential or valuable as a means to the acquisition or retention of wealth; (3) wealth and power are each proper ultimate ends of national policy; (4) there is long-run harmony between these ends, although in particular circumstances it may be necessary for a time to make economic sacrifices in the interest of military security and therefore also of long-run prosperity.

The omission of any one of these four propositions results in an incorrect interpretation of mercantilist thought, while additions of other propositions would probably involve internal dispute among mercantilists. It is to be noted that no proposition is included as to the relative weight which the mercantilists attached to power and to plenty, respectively. Given the general acceptance of the existence of harmony and mutual support between the pursuit of power and the pursuit of plenty, there appears to have been little interest in what must have appeared to them to be an unreal issue. When apparent conflict between these ends did arise, however, differences in attitudes, as between persons and countries, did arise and something will be said on this matter later.

That plenty and power were universally regarded as each valuable for its own sake there is overwhelming evidence, in the contemporary writings of all kinds, and what follows is more or less a random sampling of the available evidence. In the text accompanying and interpreting the Frontispiece of Michael Drayton's poem, *Polyolbion*, 1622, there is the following passage:

Through a Triumphant Arch see Albion
  plac'd,
In Happy site, in Neptune's arms embrac'd,
In Power and Plenty, on her Cleevy Throne

In Barbier d'Aucour's *Au Roy sur le Commerce, Ode*, 1665, an early French equivalent of *Rule Britannia*, appear the following lines:

Vos vaisseaux fendant tous les airs,
Et cinglant sur toutes les Mers,
Y porteront vostre puissance;
Et ce Commerce plein d'honneur,

From Jacob Viner, "Power versus Plenty as Objectives of Foreign Policy in the Seventeenth and Eighteenth Centuries," *World Politics*, I (1948–49), 10–20. By permission of the author and the editors of *World Politics*.

Fera naistre dans vostre France,
Un flus et reflus de bon-heur.[1]

Montchrétien opens his book with this passage: "Ceux qui sont appellez au gouvernement des Estats doyvent en avoir la gloire, l'augmentation et l'enrichissement pour leur principal but." [2] Another Frenchman, writing in 1650 says:

Deux choses sont principalement necessaires pour rendre un Estat florissant; c'est assavoir le Gouvernement, & le Commerce; & comme sans celuy-là il est impossible qu'il puisse long-temps subsister; de mesme sans celuy-cy on le voit manquer de mille sortes de choses importantes à la vie, & il est impossible que les peuples acquierent de grandes richesses.[3]

John Graunt, in 1662, states that "the art of governing, and the true politiques, is how to preserve the subject in peace, and plenty." An anonymous English writer, in 1677, declares that: "The four main interests of a nation are, religion, reputation, peace, and trade. . . ." William III, in his declaration of war against France in 1689, gives as one of the reasons that Louis XIV's "forbidding the importation of a great part of the product and manufactures of our Kingdom, and imposing exorbitant customs upon the rest, are sufficient evidence of his design to destroy the trade on which the wealth and safety of this nation so much depends." In the preamble of 3 and 4 Anne, cap. 10, are the following words: "The Royal Navy, and the navigation of England, wherein, under God, the wealth, safety, and strength of this Kingdom is so much concerned, depends on the due supply of stores for the same." An English

pamphlet of 1716 on the relations with Russia, after describing the Czar as "a great and enterprizing spirit, and of a genius thoroughly politic" attributes to him and his people "an insatiable desire of opulency, and a boundless thirst for dominion." William Wood, a noted mercantilist writer, refers to the English as "a people . . . who seek no other advantages than such only as may enlarge and secure that, whereby their strength, power, riches and reputation, equally encrease and are preserved. . . . Bernard Mandeville discusses how "politicians can make a people potent, renown'd and flourishing." An anonymous English writer states in 1771 that: "Nature, reason and observation all plainly point out to us our true object and national policy, which is commerce; the inexhaustible source of wealth and power to a people." In an undated memoir of Maurepas to Louis XVI, on the commerce of France, occur the following passages: "Le commerce est la source de la félicité, de la force et de la richesse d'un état. . . . La richesse et la puissance sont les vrais intérêts d'une nation, et il n'y a que le commerce qui puisse procurer l'une et l'autre." [4]

Such evidence as the foregoing that in the age of mercantilism wealth and power were both sought for their own sakes could easily be multiplied many fold. In English literature of the period of all kinds, from poetry to official documents, the phrases "power and plenty," "wealth and strength," "profit and power," "profit and security," "peace and plenty," or their equivalents, recur as a constant refrain. Nor is there any obvious reason, given the economic and political conditions and views of the seventeenth and eighteenth centuries, why power *and* plenty should not have been the joint objectives of the patriotic citizen of the time, even if he had freed himself from the mercantilist philosophy. Adam Smith, though not a mercantilist, was speaking for mercantilists as well as for himself when

[1] Thy ships, as they fly before every breeze and speed across every ocean, shall carry with them thy power; and this most honourable commerce shall give birth in thy land of France to a ceaseless tide of prosperity.

[2] Those who are called to govern a realm should have as their chief object its greater glory, its expansion and its enrichment.

[3] Two things are chiefly necessary in order that a State may flourish: government and trade; and just as it cannot long endure without the former, so without the latter it will lack a thousand commodities indispensable to life; and its people will find it impossible to amass great wealth.

[4] Trade is the source of the happiness, the strength and the wealth of a State. . . . Wealth and power are the true advantage of a nation and only trade may secure either.

he said that "the great object of the political oeconomy of every country, is to increase the riches and power of that country."

In all the literature I have examined, I have found only one passage which is seriously embarrassing for my thesis, not because it subordinates in extreme fashion economic to political considerations, but for the reverse reason. The passage, in an anonymous and obscure pamphlet of 1754, whose authorship I have been unable to determine, is as follows:

You want not, Gentlemen, to be informed by me, that commerce is the nearest and dearest concern of your country. It is what should be the great object of public attention in all national movements, and in every negotiation we enter into with foreign powers. Our neighbours on the continent may, perhaps, wisely scheme or quarrel for an augmentation of dominions; but *Great Britain, of herself, has nothing to fight for, nothing to support, nothing to augment but her commerce.* On our foreign trade, not only our wealth but our mercantile navigation must depend; on that navigation our naval strength, the glory and security of our country.

It is much easier indeed to show that power was not the sole objective of national policy in mercantilist thought than to explain how historians ever came to assert that it was. The evidence they cite in support of this proposition is not only extremely scanty but is generally ambiguous if not wholly irrelevant to their thesis. It would be extremely difficult, I am sure, for them to cite even a single passage which unmistakably rejects wealth as a national objective worth pursuing for its own sake or unconditionally subordinates it to power as an ultimate end. It is only too probable that there has been operating here that intellectual "principle of parsimony" in the identification of causes which, whatever its serviceability in the natural sciences, has in the history of social thought worked only for ill.

Cunningham and Heckscher make much of a passage of Francis Bacon's made famous by modern scholars in which he speaks of King Henry VII "bowing the ancient policy of this estate from consideration of plenty to consideration of power" when in the interest of the navy he ordered that wines from Gascony should be imported only in English bottoms. As a fifteenth century measure, this falls outside the period of present interest, but Bacon, no doubt, put much of his own ideas, perhaps more than of Henry VII's, in his *History of the Reign of King Henry the Seventh*. It is relevant, therefore, that Bacon speaks of Henry VII as conducting war for profit, and attributes to him even over-developed economic objectives. In 1493, Henry VII had declared an embargo on all trade with the Flemish provinces because the pretender, Perkin Warbeck, was being harboured there. The embargo after a time "began to pinch the merchants of both nations very sore, which moved them by all means they could devise to affect and dispose their sovereigns respectively to open the intercourse again." Henry VII, no longer apprehensive about Warbeck, was receptive. "But that that moved him most was, that being a King that loved wealth and treasure, he could not endure to have trade sick, nor any obstruction to continue in the gate-vein, which disperseth that blood," and by the *intercursus magnus* of 1495–96 with the Archduke of Austria he negotiated the end of the trade war.

Not so frequently stated as that power and plenty are properly joint objectives of national policy but undoubtedly a pervasive element in the thought of the period is the proposition that they are also harmonious ends, each reinforcing and promoting the other. The idea is expressed in the maxim attributed to Hobbes: "Wealth is power and power is wealth." There follow some passages in which the idea is spelled out somewhat more fully: "Foreign trade produces riches, riches power, power preserves our trade and religion." "It is evident that this kingdom is wonderfully fitted by the bounty of God almighty, for a great progression in wealth and power; and that the only means to arrive at both, or either of them, is to improve and advance trade. . . ."

"For as the honesty of all governments is, so shall be their riches; and as their honour, honesty, and riches are, so will be their strength; and as their honour, honesty, riches, and strength are, so will be their trade. These are five sisters that go hand in hand, and must not be parted." "Your fleet, and your trade, have so near a relation, and such mutual influence upon each other, they cannot well be separated; your trade is the mother and nurse of your seamen; your seamen are the life of your fleet, and your fleet is the security and protection of your trade, and both together are the wealth, strength, security and glory of Britain."

"By trade and commerce we grow a rich and powerful nation, and by their decay we are growing poor and impotent. As trade and commerce enrich, so they fortify, our country."

"The wealth of the nation he [the "Patriot King"] will most justly esteem to be his wealth, the power his power, the security and the honor, his security and honor; and by the very means by which he promotes the two first, he will wisely preserve the two last."

"De la marine dépendent les colonies, des colonies le commerce, du commerce la faculté pour l'État d'entretenir de nombreuses armées, d'augmenter la population et de fournir aux entreprises les plus glorieuses et les plus utiles." [5]

George L. Beer has commented, with particular reference to the statement from Lord Haversham quoted above, that "The men of the day argued in a circle of sea power, commerce and colonies. Sea power enabled England to expand and to protect her foreign trade, while this increased commerce, in turn, augmented her naval strength." Circular reasoning this may have been, but it was not, logically at least, a "vicious circle," since under the circumstances of the time it was perfectly reasonable to maintain that wealth and power mutually supported each other, that they were, or could be made, each a means to the augmentation of the other.

In contending that for the mercantilists power and plenty were regarded as coexisting ends of national policy which were fundamentally harmonious, I do not mean that they were unaware that in specific instances economic sacrifices might have to be made in order to assume national security or victory in an aggressive war. But as a rule, if not invariably, when making this point they showed their belief that such economic sacrifices in the short run would bring economic as well as political gains in the long run. The selfishness from a patriotic point of view of taxpayers resisting wartime impositions for armament or for war was always a problem for statesmen in the age of mercantilism, and sometimes the parsimony of monarchs was also a problem. It was also necessary at times for statesmen to resist the pressure from merchants to pursue petty commercial ends which promised immediate economic gain but at the possible cost of long-run military security and therefore also of long-run national prosperity. The mercantilist, no doubt, would not have denied that if necessity should arise for choosing, all other things would have to give way to considerations of the national safety; but his practice might not rise to the level of his principles, and his doctrine would not lead him to recognize that such choice was likely to face him frequently. It is not without significance that it was an anti-mercantilist economist, Adam Smith, and not the mercantilists, who laid down the maxim that "defence is more important than opulence." A typical mercantilist might well have replied that ordinarily defense is necessary to opulence and opulence to effective defense, even if momentarily the two ends might appear to be in conflict. . . .

Queen Elizabeth was notoriously parsimonious and one of her diplomatic agents, Buckhurst, in reasoning with her in 1587 when the safety of England against the menace from Spain appeared to call for

[5] Sea-power ensures colonies, colonies ensure commerce, and commerce ensures the ability of a State to support large armies, increase population and provide for the needs of the most glorious and fruitful enterprises.

rearmament, anticipated Adam Smith's maxim:

And alwaies when kinges and kingdoms do stand in dout of daunger, their safetie is a thing so far above all price of treasure, as there shold be no sparing to bring them even into certainty of assurans.

He accordingly advised Elizabeth to

unlock all your cofers and convert your treasure for the advauncing of worthy men and for the arming of ships and men of war, that may defend you, sith princes' treasures serve only to that end and lie they never so fast nor so full in their chests, can no waies so defend them.

Statesmen frequently found it necessary to warn against endangering political ends by unwise pursuit of temporary or petty commercial gains in response to pressure from business interests. This was especially true in connection with the relations between England and France during the Seven Years' War, which to many contemporaries seemed to be conducted with too much attention to economic considerations of minor importance. Just before the outbreak of the conflict, when it was still being debated whether the issue between the two countries should be settled by economic or military means, Lord Granville was reported as "absolutely against meddling with trade — he called it, vexing your neighbours for a little muck." And in the face of the struggle itself, Mirepoix, the French Ambassador to England, is said to have commented "that it was a great pity to cut off so many heads for the sake of a few hats." In the course of controversy over the Newfoundland fisheries after the ending of hostilities, in 1763, Choiseul appealed to Halifax: "mais pour l'amour de Dieu, ne laissons pas des querrelles de pêcheurs dégénérer en querelles de nations."

To some extent this point of view may have been a reflection of a certain disdain for trade in general which was beginning to affect the aristocratic class who con-ducted the foreign relations of the time. It would be a mistake, however, to explain it in terms of basic disregard for economic considerations, rather than as belief that the pursuit of temporary and minor economic benefits should not be permitted to dominate foreign policy. Such is the position of John Mitchell, who makes clear elsewhere that "power and prosperity" are the proper ends of policy:

It is well known, that our colonies in America are rather more under the tuition and influence of the merchants in Britain, than the government perhaps, and that all public measures relating to them are very much influenced by the opinions of our merchants about them. But the only things that they seem to attend to are the profits of trade. . . . This, it is true, is necessary to be considered likewise, but it is not the only thing to be attended to. The great thing to be considered by all states is power and dominion, as well as trade. Without that to support and protect our trade, it must soon be at an end.

While mercantilist doctrine, moreover, put great stress on the importance of national economic interests, it put equally great stress on the possibility of lack of harmony between the special economic interests of the individual merchants or particular business groups or economic classes, on the one hand, and the economic interest of the commonwealth as a whole, on the other. Refusal to give weight to *particular* economic interests, therefore, must never be identified with disregard for the national economic interest as they conceived it, in interpreting the thought of the mercantilists. In human affairs, moreover, there is always room for divergence between dogma and practice, between principles and the actual behavior of those who profess them. It is doctrine, and not practice, which is the main concern here. The task of ascertaining how much or how little they corresponded in the age of mercantilism, and what were the forces which caused them to deviate, is the difficult duty of the historian, in whose hands I gladly leave it.

IV. MERCANTILISM—SOME RECENT VIEWS

Mercantilism and the Colonies

LAWRENCE A. HARPER

Lawrence Averell Harper (born 1901), a graduate of the University of California and Columbia, has been professor of history at Berkeley since 1947. Author of *The English Navigation Laws, a Seventeenth-Century Experiment in Social Engineering*, and several papers, he is also a practicing customs lawyer.

THE TERM "mercantilism" is one of those words which have different meanings for different people. On the one hand, George Louis Beer claimed that English mercantilism was a well-balanced system designed for the benefit of the colonies as well as the mother country, and on the other, Sir William Ashley declared that the regulations of English mercantilism were either pious formulas nullified in the actual world of commerce by fraud and evasion, or merely a codification of commercial habits which would have been followed in any case. . . . [We] shall reject Beer's claim that there was no exploitation and accept the statements of the mercantilists themselves that they planned to exploit the colonies for the benefit of the mother country. We shall deny the Ashley view that there was no actual regulation and conclude from more recent studies of the evidence that the English laws did regulate trade and commerce.

These two conclusions provide us with a working definition of English mercantilism in its colonial aspects. It had as its purpose, exploitation, and as its means, regulation. Both phases of the problem, exploitation *and* regulation, are important. To understand the relationship of mercantilism and the Revolution we must not only analyse the extent to which the colonists were exploited but also consider the skill with which they were regulated.

An analysis of how the colonists were exploited is no easy task, as any one knows who has struggled with the many statutory ambiguities involved. The calculations involved in estimating the burdens placed upon the colonial economy are complicated. They call for arithmetical computations involving duties, preferences, or drawbacks of such odd amounts as 1s. 10d. and 15 16/75 of a twentieth of a penny per pound of tobacco. They run afoul of complicated analyses of costs and close decisions about the incidence of taxation. . . .

All that can be attempted here is to state the conclusions and indicate the grounds upon which they are based. We can, however, simplify our analysis of the mercantilist code which exploited the colonies by dividing it into four parts: first, the basic provisions concerning the trans-Atlantic trade; second, the supplementary measures restricting manufactures; third, the subsidiary rules with reference to the American trade; and fourth, the much discussed

From Lawrence A. Harper, "Mercantilism and the American Revolution," *Canadian Historical Review* (1942), 1–15. Reprinted by permission of the University of Toronto Press and the author.

measures enacted after the French and Indian War.

In examining the first part, we find that the basic provisions concerning the trans-Atlantic trade placed a heavy burden upon the colonies. By means of the Navigation Acts England attempted both to keep foreign vessels out of the colonies and to enable English merchants to share in the more profitable parts of the trans-Atlantic trade. The enumeration of key colonial exports in various Acts from 1660 to 1766 and the Staple Act of 1663 hit at colonial trade both coming and going. The Acts required the colonies to allow English middlemen to distribute such crops as tobacco and rice and stipulated that if the colonies would not buy English manufactures, at least they should purchase their European goods in England. The greatest element in the burden laid upon the colonies was not the taxes assessed. It consisted in the increased costs of shipment, trans-shipment, and middleman's profits arising out of the requirement that England be used as an *entrepôt*.

The burdens were somewhat lightened by legislation favouring the colonies, but not as much as usually alleged. The suppression of tobacco production in England, for example, was comparatively unimportant to the colonies since the great quantities of colonial tobacco re-exported caused its price to be determined by a world rather than an English market. Moreover, the motive was not goodwill for the colonists but fiscal, since the heavy revenues derived from tobacco could be collected more easily at the waterfront than upon the farm. Likewise, although colonial shipbuilders and shipowners approved the clauses of the Navigation Acts which eliminated Dutch rivals, they did not need such protection. They had managed to carry cargoes and to build ships which could be sold in the world market before the laws were enacted and they continued to do so after the Revolution. The fact is that colonial shipowners suffered, directly, and colonial shipbuilders, indirectly, under the Navigation Acts since

other clauses enabled English shipowners (as contrasted with American) to carry eighty per cent of the trade between the British Isles and the Thirteen Colonies whereas they carried only twenty per cent after the Revolution.

Similarly the drawbacks, bounties, and tariff preferences, of which we are so often reminded, did not materially offset the burdens placed upon the trans-Atlantic trade. The drawbacks paid by English customs authorities on foreign products re-exported to the colonies should not be listed as a benefit to the colonies. There would have been no duties to be drawn back except for the requirement that the colonists purchase their European goods in England. The portion of the duties which England retained, while less than it might have been, was obviously greater than nothing at all. Likewise, *bounties paid upon English manufactures* exported to the colonies, were of advantage to the English producer, who received them whether his goods were exported to the colonies or anywhere else, rather than of benefit to the colonial consumer who otherwise would, and often did, buy competitive European goods.

On the other hand, however, the bounties paid upon colonial products were of real advantage to the colonies. They sustained the growth of indigo in South Carolina, did much to foster the development of naval stores in North Carolina, encouraged the lumber industry in New England, and at the end of the colonial period averaged more than £65,000 a year for the Thirteen Colonies alone. Similarly the preferences granted colonial products were beneficial in so far as they operated. Although they had no effect upon such commodities as tobacco and rice and their effect upon other commodities is somewhat uncertain, colonial raw silk, naval stores, and lumber definitely benefited. Yet the total sum represented by such preferences was never great and it is doubtful whether the benefit the Thirteen Colonies thus derived amounted to even one-twentieth of that obtained by the British West Indian planters who in the year

1773 alone, pocketed £446,000, thanks to a preferential rate which enabled their sugar to hold the English market despite a five-shilling-per-hundred-weight differential in price.

The uncertainties underlying many of our calculations do not permit an exact statement, but judging from calculations for the year 1773, it would seem that after all proper allowances have been made for bounties and other preferences, the net burden imposed upon the Thirteen Colonies by the restraints upon the trans-Atlantic trade was between two million and seven million dollars a year. . . .

When we turn to the second part of our discussion, the supplementary measures restricting manufacture, we find a difference of opinion concerning the effect of English restrictions upon manufacturing wool, hats, and iron. The earlier tendency was to dismiss the regulations as immaterial, but recently some have swung the pendulum to the other extreme and argue that the restraints were very important. Neither extreme appears to accord with the facts. In the case of hats, proximity to the source of supply of furs and the comparatively simple process of manufacturing had led to the development of an industry which appears to have been injured by the legislation, but the hat industry played only a minor part in the total economy. Woollen manufactures were, of course, much more important, but there is much evidence to indicate that the English prohibitions had little material effect. The colonies found that they were handicapped by an inadequate supply of good wool when they tried to develop homespun goods at the time of the Revolution — and even as late as 1791 Hamilton found that an adequate supply of labour was one of the chief stumbling blocks to his programme for encouraging industry. It required an embargo, a war, and a protective tariff before large-scale woollen manufacturing began to develop, and it did not pass beyond the household stage until many years after being freed of English mercantilism — which, incidentally,

had never forbidden the manufacture of homespun for domestic use or local distribution.

In the case of iron manufactures the British legislation encouraged the development of pig and bar iron and tried to discourage the manufacture of more advanced forms, but in both respects the influence of the legislation is doubtful. Because of the proximity of iron ore to forests America had a great advantage in producing crude iron, before coke replaced charcoal, and probably did not need legislative encouragement. With such an advantage in producing crude iron it was only natural that some more advanced iron articles would be produced in the colonies, whatever thorough-going mercantilists might dream about having the crude iron sent over to England and having it returned in the form of pots, pans, and other manufactures.

The various disallowances of colonial laws which were intended to foster colonial manufacturing further illustrate the English intention of discouraging it but, despite that intent, English mercantilism as a whole probably had a greater tendency to promote than to hinder colonial industry. The colonies' most dangerous industrial competitors were in many respects, not the English, but the Dutch, the Germans, and other Europeans — to say nothing of the natives of India — against whose competition the provisoes of the Staple Act of 1663 provided a very useful tariff barrier. Moreover, the large sums which mercantilism withheld from the colonies reduced their available cash, and probably forced many colonists to use homespun or other American products instead of buying British.

The third point of our inquiry into colonial exploitation by England should not detain us long. Until the Molasses Act of 1733 the inter-American trade had been left virtually alone except for the requirement that the English colonies trade in English or colonial ships. Even after 1733, the prohibitive duties on foreign sugar, molasses, and rum were usually evaded. Such evasion required bribery, fraud, or concealment which probably served as a mildly protective tariff in favour of the British sugar islands, but the prices quoted in the Thirteen Colonies for sugar, molasses, and rum do not indicate that the legislation had any radical effect upon the trade.

The fourth part of our inquiry — that relating to the period after 1763 — is a different matter. The researches of Schlesinger and others have demonstrated how the British measures of that period aroused the resentment of the merchants who unleashed an avalanche of agitation which soon went beyond their control. The agitation was not directed toward revolution at first, but agitation by its very nature promotes conditions favourable for revolution — and revolution followed as a natural sequence. Yet, conceding all the irritation thus aroused, we must still face the questions: Were the measures unduly exploitive? Did they fundamentally upset the economic equilibrium? Were they fatal ills which would inevitably lead to the death of the Empire, or merely minor upsets from which the Empire might have recovered — granted otherwise favourable conditions and good luck?

In reviewing the period it does not seem fair to blame British mercantilism for prescribing regulations which were demanded by the circumstances of the time. The British currency and land policies seem to fall under this category. The restrictions upon paper money undoubtedly distressed those who lacked funds, but they merely affirmed a truth which Americans had to learn from sad experience — that in the eighteenth century at least, no political alchemy could transmute paper into gold. Similarly the Proclamation of 1763 and the Quebec Act of 1774 essentially concerned imperial problems and American imitation of the policy after independence was not mere flattery but a tribute to its inherent soundness. The measures disappointed those who had hoped to acquire fortunes from land speculation, but what else could the British have done? Neither they nor

the United States government after them could allow private individuals to stir up trouble by moving into Indian territory before the way had been prepared for settlement by negotiations which extinguished the Indians' claims to the area. In view of the British debt it was merely good fiscal policy to charge for the land, and the prices and terms of sale proposed by the British mercantilists seem very reasonable when compared with the prices and terms adopted by the federal government after 1787. And what solution did the Thirteen States themselves find for the conflicting claims to the territory west of the Alleghanies except to create a new governmental unit?

To one who frankly does not profess to be an expert on the point, it is difficult to understand how British mercantilism discriminated materially against the colonists. It is true that in the manoeuvering for land grants, British interests sometimes clashed with colonial interests, but we hear fully as much about clashes between different colonial groups. Both the small frontiersmen and the big speculators were charged more for land than they were accustomed to pay, but it was not as much as they were to be charged by the United States government thereafter. In the readjustments which accompanied the establishment of the new policies the fur traders of the Thirteen Colonies suffered somewhat because of the machinations of British opponents but their loss was not great, and in any event by the Revolutionary period trade in furs formed only a negligible fraction of the colonial economy.

The pre-Revolutionary taxation measures, however, are a different matter, and one for which British mercantilism must bear full responsibility. Yet in analysing the figures we find that the average annual revenue raised by the Sugar Acts, the Townshend Acts, and all the other taxes collected in the Thirteen Colonies by the British government amounted to only £31,000. This sum barely exceeded the indirect taxes which were collected on colonial merchandise passing through England.

Moreover, both the taxes collected indirectly in England and directly in the colonies failed to equal the bounties which the British government was paying to the colonies — to say nothing of the advantages which they were deriving from preferential duties on their shipments to England. More interesting still, calculated on an annual per capita basis, the taxes collected during the Revolutionary period directly in the colonies and indirectly in England, totalled less than one-seventh of the taxes assessed at the beginning of the century.

Yet even though the amount of taxation was not great, we must consider the possibility that the form of its assessment detrimentally affected colonial interests. The Tea Act, for one, definitely injured the illicit trade in tea by so reducing the price of the legal article that it lessened, if it did not eliminate, the profit from smuggling. However unfair smugglers may have thought such tactics, they can hardly be said to have injured the economy of the country — especially since tea was not a pivotal commodity.

Molasses, the rum which was made from it, and the provision trade which accompanied it, however, were vital factors in colonial economy, and historians have often called attention to their importance in such books as *Rum, Romance, and Rebellion*. The Sugar Act of 1764 served notice that the British government intended to make its regulations effective when it lowered the duty on foreign sugar and molasses and prohibited the importation of foreign rum entirely. The provisions concerning sugar and rum were comparatively immaterial since no great quantities were imported, but the duty of 3d. per gallon on molasses was another matter, since literally millions of gallons came from the foreign West Indies. Many feared that the trade could not bear a tax of 3d. per gallon, and in response to their pleas the duty was reduced in 1766 to 1d. per gallon and the tax was assessed on both British and foreign molasses. The excitement aroused by these taxes leads one to look for evidence of the havoc which

they wrought in trade, but an examination of the wholesale prices of molasses does not disclose any noticeable change attributable to the legislation. And if we carry our investigations further we find that the tax which the federal government placed and kept upon imports of molasses after 1790 almost equaled the 3d. per gallon placed upon foreign molasses in 1764 and materially exceeded the 1d. duty retained after 1766. In brief, whatever the connection between rum and romance, the statistics of colonial trade disclose no correlation between rum and rebellion.

In so far as the statistics can be followed, the correlation between wine and rebellion is much closer. The Sugar Act of 1764 had also placed a duty upon wines which gave those imported by way of Britain a preferential rate of £3 per ton. The preference was not sufficient to enable the English to capture the trade in Madeira wine, but it enabled them to gain a flourishing trade in port which previously had been negligible. Yet such an infringement of colonial taste hardly seems to justify a revolt — especially when we note that the quantity involved was not large, and that by the post-Revolutionary period Americans preferred port and other wines to Madeira.

Thus, an analysis of the economic effects of British mercantilism fails to establish its exploitive aspects as the proximate cause of the Revolution. The only measures which afforded a sufficient economic grievance were the *entrepôt* provisions of the Navigation Acts, which governed the trans-Atlantic trade. They helped to create a fundamental economic unbalance, but cannot be connected directly with the Revolution. The colonists had lived under them for more than a century without desiring independence and even in the Revolutionary period with few exceptions the *entrepôt* provisions were accepted as the mother country's due for the protection which she afforded. In fact, the official representatives of the colonies were willing to guarantee the British commercial system provided that the measures of political taxation were withdrawn. If there were any inexorable economic forces which were inevitably drawing the colonies toward revolution, they are hard to detect and the colonists were unaware of them.

Anyone who maintains that the Revolution resulted from the inevitable clash of competing capitalisms must reckon with several points: That burdens upon the trans-Atlantic trade were proportionately greater at the beginning of the eighteenth century than in 1776; that the restraints of the land and currency policies were basically the same as those prescribed by the federal government; and that after 1766 the taxes laid on molasses by Britain were less than those imposed by the United States after 1790. He should also explain why the surplus colonial capital alleged to be bursting its confines did not venture into the manufacturing enterprises which the law did not prohibit; why the colonists did not finance their own middlemen in England; and, finally, why they did not pay their debts. If by a clash of expanding capitalism is meant that colonists with money were irritated because their freedom of action was restrained by outside regulation, one must immediately concede that the charge is justified; but such colonial resentment seems more properly classified as a political rather than an economic factor. It is merely an old point dressed in new garb and was better expressed by John Adams when he declared that the American Revolution began when the first plantation was settled.

When we turn, however, from the economic effects of mercantilism to its regulatory aspects, we are faced with a different story. We can establish a direct correlation between mercantilism and the Revolution. Although earlier English regulations had been reasonably satisfactory the regulatory technique of the British government under George III was pitifully defective. As a mother country, Britain had much to learn. Any modern parents' magazine could have told George III's ministers that the one mistake not to make is to take a stand and then to yield to howls of anguish. It was a mistake which the British government made repeatedly. It placed a duty of 3d. per gallon on molasses, and when it encountered opposition, reduced it to 1d. It provided for a Stamp Act and withdrew it in the face of temper tantrums. It provided for external taxes to meet the colonial objections and then yielded again by removing all except one. When finally it attempted to enforce discipline it was too late. Under the circumstances, no self-respecting child — or colonist — would be willing to yield.

Moreover, British reforming zeal came at a very bad time. The colonists were in a particularly sensitive state due to the postwar deflation and the economic distress which accompanied it. The British also attempted to exert unusual control at a time when the removal of the French from Canada had minimized the colonists' dependence upon Britain. Most important of all, the reforms followed one another too rapidly.

In social reform, irritation often is to be measured not so much by what a regulation attempts to achieve as by the extent to which it changes established habits. The early history of English mercantilism itself offers a good illustration of the point. Bitter complaints came from Virginia and Barbados when tobacco and sugar were first enumerated because those colonies had become accustomed to conditions of comparatively free trade, whereas few or no complaints were heard from Jamaica which had developed under the restrictive system. The mercantilist system was geared for leisurely operation and before George III's reign succeeded by virtue of that fact. Its early restraints led to Bacon's rebellion in Virginia but fortunately for the mother country the pressure against New England was deferred until the next decade when it, too, led to an explosion in the form of revolt against Andros. These uprisings were separated both geographically and chronologically so that neither attained dangerous proportions, and both were followed by a reasonably satisfactory settlement of at least some of the colonial grievances.

During the Revolutionary era, however, the tempo of reform was not leisurely. Doubtless all the colonists were not irritated by any one British reform, but each individual had his own feeling of grievance which enabled him to agree fervently with the complaints of others against British policy and thus add to the heated tempers of the time. The politician who objected to the political implications in taxation reforms found an audience in the land speculators and frontiersmen who complained that the colonists were being deprived of the reward of their blood and suffering by the Proclamation of 1763 and the Quebec Act of 1774. Debtors and inflationists chimed in to tell of the iniquities of the Currency Act; lawyers and printers could not forget the threat to their interests in the Stamp Act. On Sundays the preachers thundered against the dangers of popery in Quebec and voiced their fear that Britain planned to establish an Anglican Church in the colonies. The merchant was always ready to explain not merely how harmful British taxes were to colonial economy, but how irksome were the new administrative rules and regulations. Such chronological and geographical barriers as existed were overcome and a community of antagonisms was maintained by the Committees of Correspondence and other agitators, but such revolutionary forces could not have succeeded if the different elements of the colonies had not recently experienced a mutual sense of grievance.

In short, many of the misunderstandings which have arisen in connection with mercantilism and the American Revolution have grown out of the failure to distinguish between the two phases of mercantilism: exploitation and regulation. The fact that the colonists were exploited by English mercantilism does not necessarily mean that mercantilism caused the American Revolution. Economic forces are not magnets which inexorably move men in predetermined patterns. For better or for worse, men try to regulate their economic as well as their political destiny. A large part of governmental activity consists in attempting to mould economic conduct and to minimize the friction which results from clashes or constraints. English mercantilism was such an attempt. It succeeded rather well in minimizing friction until 1764. For the next decade it bungled badly, and the penalty was the loss of the Thirteen Colonies.

The Liberal Elements in Mercantilism

William D. Grampp (born 1914) is professor of economics at the University of Illinois, Chicago Circle, and his major interest is in the history of economic thought. He is coeditor (with Emanuel Weiler) of *Economic Policy: Readings in Political Economy* (Homewood, Ill., 1954) and is the author of *The Manchester School* (Stanford, 1960), and *Economic Liberalism* (2 volumes; New York, 1965).

THE PERIOD of mercantilism in England extended from roughly 1500 to 1750, and it is customary to apply that word both to the economic writings of the period and to its economic practices. It is also customary to describe mercantilism as the antithesis of liberal, or classical, economic doctrine. Adam Smith used some of his strongest invective against it, and since his time mercantilism has been thoroughly condemned by liberal economists because its practices were the very kind of interference which they always have regarded as useless, unwise, or mischievous.

By reasoning from the actual practices of the mercantilist states, economists and historians usually have supposed that the doctrines of the period of mercantilism were a justification of its institutions. It is common in studies of mercantilism for the author to explain, say, the restriction of imports by referring both to the tariff duties of the age and to the concurrent doctrine of a favorable balance of trade, or for him to move freely among expressions of public officials, laws, economic tracts and discourses, and to suppose that because particular controls were exercised, like price fixing, they must have been justified in the economic writing of the time. No one, of course, would write of recent economic policy this way. It would be unthinkable to describe the New Deal by an indiscriminate reference to the works of Keynes and Hansen and to the public papers of Franklin D. Roosevelt and the private memoranda of Harry Hopkins and always to suppose that whatever the state did or wanted to do found its rationalization in economic doctrine.

When studies of mercantilism use a method of this kind, they leave an impression with the reader that in many ways is distressingly wrong. He must be led to think that because the mercantilist states did not believe in the market as the mechanism for discharging the economic functions of society, the economists of the age held the same belief and were in favor of the intricate kind of regulation which was practiced. More indeed than this is implied. If the practitioners of mercantilism did not understand prices, money, foreign trade, and other matters, it follows that the economists also were wanting in a knowledge of these matters. Especially is it implied that the mercantilists did not understand the mechanism by which the economic problem is solved in a free society and that this knowledge was the signal discovery of classical economics. From this it must be concluded that the mercantilist

Reprinted by permission of the publishers from William Grampp, "The Liberal Elements in English Mercantilism," *The Quarterly Journal of Economics,* LXVI (1952), 465–501. Cambridge, Mass.: Harvard University Press, Copyright, 1952, by the President and Fellows of Harvard College.

writers were particularly deficient because they did not understand how the price system directs resources to particular employments and causes the product to be distributed in a certain way.

None of these impressions about mercantilist *doctrine,* as distinct from mercantilist *practice,* is correct. Yet they are unavoidable if the doctrine and the practice are thought to be parts of a unified system. It is the purpose of this essay to re-examine the ideas expressed by the mercantilist writers of England between about 1550 and 1750 in order to show that the mercantilists anticipated many important elements of classical economic doctrine, including the classical conception of self-interest, the price mechanism, the mutual advantage in exchange, and the place of the state in the economic organization. . . .

I

What did the mercantilist writers believe was the objective of economic policy? What were their measures of control meant to achieve? The answer must be taken from diverse writings of a period covering some two centuries. In generalizing from them, there is the danger of supposing them to be more consistent than they actually are, just in order to make the question manageable. But the hazard is worth taking. Mercantilism was an important stage in the development of economic ideas, and a fresh approach to it may aid in making it more comprehensible.

Had the mercantilist writers been asked for an explicit statement of their objective, they undoubtedly would have said it was to create a strong and secure England. Although their motives were mixed (as most writers' are) the principal motive was the national interest. It was not this, however, which made mercantilism different from classical economics. The classical economists also were nationalists; they valued the political and military interest of England above all things and were ready to sacrifice efficiency and even justice in return for greater national power. The title of Smith's

work describes the purpose of his policy of laissez faire. The purpose of John Hales's policy is also indicated by the title of his work, written about 1549, *A Discourse of the Common Weal of This Realm of England.* Now the word "nationalism" is a piece of intensional language, and when applied to the economists, has to be shorn of its inflammatory connotation. They were not like Lord Copper, who stood for "strong mutually antagonistic governments everywhere, self-sufficiency at home, self-assertion abroad." Rather they were devoted to God, St. George, and particularly England.

What separated the mercantilists from the liberal economists was their different means of advancing the national interest. The mercantilists believed the latter required a prosperous, fully employed, and growing economy. The connection between power and wealth was expressed about 1548 in the *Pleasant Poeyse of Princelie Practise* by Sir William Forest:

> For kings of their commons sometime must aid true.
> The more therefore the public weal doth afflow;
> The more is their wealth: this reason proveth now.

Among the conditions necessary for a growing economy the mercantilists cited: a brisk trade, adequate domestic spending, a proper wage and price structure, a particular distribution of income, an excess of exports over imports, a diligent and obedient working class, security of private property, the elimination of monopoly, the full utilization of agricultural lands, an adequate money supply, a low rate of interest, and the full employment of the labor force.

The greatest attention was given to the money supply, spending, and employment. Spending, or in today's language, effective demand, and employment were regarded as mutually determined: whatever changed one would change the other in the same direction. The money supply in some writings was made a determinant of spending while in others it was not directly related to spending. To most of the mercantilists, the condition of national prosperity was an amount of spending sufficient to maintain full employment, and these writers subordinated the accumulation of bullion and other methods of increasing the money supply to the position of determinants of spending. Full employment was taken to be a measure of the quantity of goods produced by the economy, and full employment was the economic objective of mercantilist policy, as distinct from its practical objective, which was national power.

* * *

Contemporary writers indicated how important they felt full employment to be by their frequent assertion that the wealth of the nation depended on its "labor"; by the significance they attached to the size of the population; by the common statement that the advantage of trade was in the numbers it employed; by the grave concern expressed over the extent of unemployment, idleness, and poverty, in the numerous remedies by which these problems were to be eliminated and the productivity of labor was to be increased. Most of the measures of policy can be explained more simply and completely by assuming that full employment was the mercantilists' objective than by supposing that some other purpose directed their ideas.

It is, however, possible to assume that the amount of "trade" was the keystone of policy, if one uses the word, as the mercantilists usually did, to include *all* economic activity. Their designs for "a brisk trade" then become methods of assuring the maximum amount of productive effort which is what full employment is also meant to provide. But the word, "trade," has a narrower meaning in modern usage, denoting one aspect of the distributive process, and therefore its use can mislead one into thinking the mercantilists ignored manufacturing, agriculture, shipping, and other industries, which in fact they did not. Moreover, many of the mercantilists'

ideas can be related more directly to the amount of employment than to the amount of trade (as their ideas about psychological motivation). Of course, the words "full employment" also can be misleading, but less so, I believe, than any others which can describe the objective of mercantilist policy.

The objective was not, as often supposed, the accumulation of bullion, a favorable balance of trade, the advancement of private interests, the subordination of the working class, low interest rates, the elevation of trade at the expense of other industries. Some of these considerations were means to the end of full employment; some were not entertained by the majority of writers at all. A few of the mercantilists may have confused money with wealth and so made bullionism an end. None of the considerations occupied as important a place in the doctrine as full employment did, and none serves so well to unify the particular measures of control which were proposed.

Once full employment is taken as the objective of mercantilist policy, that policy's difference from liberal policy narrows considerably. Although the difference is not eliminated, it is much less than if one supposes that the objective of mercantilism was, say, a favorable balance of trade, which the liberals never could have accepted as an end.

As many of the commentaries assume a favorable balance of trade to be the objective of mercantilist policy, it perhaps is necessary to explain why that view is not accepted in this essay. If this had been the mercantilists' objective, it is unlikely that they would have given much attention to the money supply, employment, spending, domestic trade, and to other matters which have only an indirect connection, if any at all, with a favorable trade balance. Moreover they would have emphasized a restriction of imports at least as much as an increase in exports, since by either method a favorable balance could have been realized. One can try, of course, to explain away

their doctrine by assuming they were ignorant and illogical. But this does them less
than justice. It also leaves one puzzled over
why later generations have studied what
they said so closely, if they were merely
unenlightened and unreasonable scribblers.

It is my opinion that their desire to maintain a favorable balance of trade was based
on the assumption that England would be
able to increase employment by exporting
more than it imported — an assumption
which is plausible in the short run. In the
long run, the policy would have supported
domestic employment if England had in-
vested its net receipts abroad; and it is of
interest that some mercantilists, like
Thomas Mun (1630), recommended this
practice.

II

In order to achieve full employment, the
mercantilists proposed a variety of measures. Most of the measures have often
been called wonderful examples of what
an economy should not undertake. However, they become sensible if related to the
objective of policy. The measures can be
grouped into those which affected: (1) the
total spending of the economy, (2) prices,
wages, and the distribution of income, (3)
interest rates, and (4) the supply of labor.
The measures in the first three groups were
meant to increase employment mainly by
increasing the demand for labor while those
in the fourth group were meant to increase
the labor supply.

(1) Most of the mercantilists believed
the economy would prosper if there was the
maximum amount of spending by individuals, business enterprise, and foreigners, to
which Petty added the government. Although most mercantilists thought of spending on exports as the principal support of
employment, some noted that spending in
wholly domestic markets was also important. Petty noted that there were circumstances which justified public extravagance,
because it put money into the hands of the
tradesman; he did, however, think it more
prudent for the state, whenever possible, to
use its fiscal powers to direct spending to
capital goods (or encourage investment).
Barbon observed that covetousness (a high
propensity to save) reduced consumption,
income, government revenues, and employment. He submitted that the most powerful stimulant to trade, even though he
thought it wasteful in itself, was spending
on goods which quickly became obsolete.
Defoe believed the economy prospered
when consumers spent a large proportion
of their income, although he urged the
tradesman himself to be frugal in order
that trade and employment would be secure. North was less concerned with the
solvency of the tradesman than with the
state of all trade, which, he said, will decline if "the consumption fails, as when
men by reason of poverty, do not spend so
much in their houses as formerly they did."
Many of the mercantilists were alarmed by
the hoarding of gold and silver, and showed
their alarm by frequent aspersions on individuals who fancied "plate" and on those
who were covetous. North deferred to the
common view of hoarding to the extent of
defending a miser by saying that even he
spends occasionally and when he does
"those he sets on work benefit by their
being employed."

However, it was foreign trade more than
domestic trade which interested the mercantilists, because they believed it contributed more to employment, to the nation's
wealth, and to its power. The writers *after*
1600 stressed the inflationary effect of an
excess of exports over imports and the con-
sequent increase in employment produced
by inflation. They reasoned that a favorable balance of trade brought gold and
silver to England, that the greater money
supply caused spending to increase, and
that the greater spending would increase
employment. Some viewed exports more
directly and naively, thinking that greater
exports meant greater employment. Few of
the mercantilists distinguished carefully between the short- and long-run effects of a
favorable trade balance, a deficiency, however, which would be more noteworthy if

it were not that many of their critics also failed to make the distinction carefully.

In order to secure a favorable balance, the mercantilists proposed their familiar commercial policy: duties on imports, with rebates on raw materials used in making exports; the prohibition of certain imported goods; the removal of export duties; subsidies and other assistance to the export industries; monopoly grants to certain joint stock companies engaged in foreign trade; a prohibition of the export of coin and bullion; and an aggressive foreign policy by which England would help its exporters capture markets from their competitors.

The mercantilists who wrote *before* 1600 believed a favorable balance would enable England to accumulate bullion for war purposes. For this reason Hales regarded the export industries as most valuable to the nation, saying: "I would have them most preferred and cherished that bring in most commodity and treasure to the country," commodity and treasure being synonyms here. . . .

(2) The mercantilists' ideas about wages and prices were related to employment in four ways. One view was that wages determined export prices and the amount of exports, and hence determined spending and employment. Another was that the relationship between money wages and prices, or real wages, determined the distribution of income which in turn affected the amount of spending and employment. A third was that selling prices determined the amount of spending and employment. A fourth was that real wages determined the quantity of labor supplied. . . .

(3) In addition to achieving full employment by measures related to spending and to wages and prices, some of the mercantilists wished to use the rate of interest for this purpose. There was more agreement about the rate of interest than about the correct wage and price policy but less than about the importance of adequate spending. . . .

In addition to believing that it determined the rate of interest, there were two other reasons why the mercantilists attended so closely to the money supply. One was the belief that for any given amount of trade there was an appropriate supply of money and that as the supply increased there would be an increase in trade and employment. In this conception, a change in the money supply was thought to operate directly on the spending rather than indirectly through changing the interest rate. . . .

The other reason for the mercantilists' attention to money was the belief that an accumulation of bullion could be desirable in itself. . . .

(4) There was a final group of measures by which the mercantilists meant to increase employment. It consisted of means of increasing the quantity of labor supplied (the relationship of real wages to which was explained above), of increasing the labor supply, and of increasing the productivity of labor. That the mercantilists looked at employment from the supply as well as demand side of the market indicates their policy sought to increase the quantity of resources and was not a make-shift for creating jobs.

Their methods of increasing the labor force are harsh by today's standards and often are interpreted as revealing an animosity toward the lower classes. Those who interpret the mercantilists this way usually imply that the classical economists had a more enlightened view of the working class. Certainly more sympathy was expressed by the classicists; there was less carping, less preaching of the early-to-bed, early-to-rise variety, and there was more tolerance of distinctively human behavior. But when all this is said, there still remains the fact that the classical economists did not make any important proposals to redistribute income or otherwise to ameliorate the condition of the lower classes except to urge that the best hope for them, as for all other classes, was the steady growth of national output, a goal which the mercantilists just as persistently sought although by somewhat different means.

Actually, most of the mercantilist labor policy came from the assumption that self-interest governs individual conduct, an assumption as fully entertained today as it was two and three hundred years ago. The principle which directed the mercantilists to believe that the unemployed should receive only a subsistence allowance is no different from that which leads modern economists to believe unemployment compensation should be set much below prevailing wages in order that the idle shall not come to prefer leisure to work. The point was made very clear by J. S. Mill, who argued that the best way to treat the poor is to make them wish they were rich.

The mercantilist labor policy consisted of measures to increase the population; to increase the size of the labor force within a given population, in numbers of workers and in the amount of work supplied by each laborer; and to increase the productivity of the labor force. In order to increase the population some writers proposed that subsidies be given to large families; and occasionally they attached the ingenious scheme of financing the subsidies by a tax on bachelors (which makes one wonder what would have happened had the subsidies been successful). Other methods were to encourage the immigration of skilled workers and tradesmen which, it was believed, would be easier if there were greater religious tolerance. The percentage of the labor force to the total population was to be increased by bringing children into employment. Petty estimated that if all those between six and sixteen were employed the national income of England would be increased by five million pounds (about the year 1662). Almost all mercantilists considered ways of bringing more persons into the labor force. They wished to reduce the enlistments in the army and navy and to direct men into gainful employment, to turn criminals to legitimate activity, and, above all, to rehabilitate the poor and indigent whom circumstances or choice had deprived of the will to work. . . .

In order to increase the amount of work offered, it was proposed that the state remove the many distractions which kept the workers from being industrious. Drinking was the first to be attended to. According to Defoe:

In English ale their dear enjoyment lies,
For which they'll starve themselves
      and families.
An Englishman will fairly drink as much
As will maintain two families of Dutch.

Tucker would have done away with cockpits, skittle-alleys, stages for cudgel playing, making book on horse races, the selling of liquor, cakes, fruit, "or any like temptations to draw people together" and away from their jobs. Other mercantilists asked for sumptuary control, because they thought the wearing of ribbons and ruffles and the drinking of tea made workers prideful and lazy. It is interesting that such proposals hardly ever expressed the fear of insubordination turning into sedition. It was sloth which alarmed the mercantilists.

For the purpose of increasing labor productivity, it was proposed the workers be shown that industry, skill, and enterprise were to their advantage. Rewards were to be given for excellence of work, some in money, some in the form of distinction. Industrious and skilled immigrants were to be attracted to England in order to set an example to native workers. Children were to be trained to the habit of work from an early age, and older persons were to be shown in a variety of ways the rewards from industry. In his program for improving the poor, Tucker asked that courts be formed in each district to supervise the working class, each court to be presided over by "Guardians of the Morals of the Manufacturing Poor." By precept, inducement, and punishment, the poor would be transformed into a national asset. One of the rewards was to be "a good book" stamped in gold on one side with "The Hand of the Diligent Maketh Rich" and on the other, "To the Praise of Them that Do Well."

The labor policy of the mercantilists was a logical derivation of their economic psychology. Almost all believed there were three factors which directed individuals to economic activity: the stimulus given by physical environment, the desire of men to emulated their betters (a desire partly created by social environment), and the eagerness for pecuniary rewards. It was believed that men were the more industrious, the more difficult were the conditions in which they lived: the climate, soil fertility, the national wealth in relation to the population. The less favorable was their environment, the more likely they were to become rich.

Pestlethwayt summarized the idea by saying, "The greatest industry has ever been the effect of the greatest necessity."

The second factor which made men industrious was their desire to emulate those above them in social position and income. Petty wrote that men always seek to excel, and when placed together, as in large cities, their emulative instinct becomes all the keener, evoking their industry, increasing spending, and providing opportunity for still greater industry. Other writers, like Defoe, doubted the beneficence of emulation, believing it often made men imprudent, but they admitted the motive was a strong one.

The third factor was the desire for monetary returns. It was thought to be the principal cause of industry, and that the greater were the money returns from a particular employment the greater usually would be the quantity of resources supplied to that employment. The idea was expressed quite early and repeated down to the end of the mercantilist period when it was carried forward by the classical economists in their doctrine of self-interest. Hales wrote that "profit or advancement nourishes every faculty; which saying is so true, that it is allowed by the common judgment of all men." The idea was expressed by other mercantilists, among them Petty, North, Davenant, and Defoe, the last of whom said, somewhat prodigally:

Gain is the tradesman's life, 'tis the essence of his being, as a qualified tradesman. Convenience, and supply of necessary things for life, were the first causes indeed of trade; but the reason and end of the tradesman is to get money: 'Tis the polestar and guide, the aim and design of all his notions; 'tis the center and point to which all his actions tend; 'tis the soul of business, the spur of industry, the wheel that turns within all wheels of his whole business, and gives motion to the rest.

What Defoe said of the tradesman (and Lamb described more economically as "the quick pulse of gain") was believed true of all in the economy and true in a special way of the worker. An increase in real wages would be accompanied by an increase in the quantity of labor supplied until real wages reached a certain amount, and if they went beyond this amount the quantity of labor supplied would decrease. The mercantilists who thought of the labor supply function in this way believed that pecuniary self-interest had less of an effect on the worker than on others in the economy; or that before the pecuniary motive could operate effectively the worker had first to become accustomed to high real wages. It had, therefore, to be reinforced by other factors. One was emulation. This trait could be exploited by placing before the working man the rewards which others had acquired by their industry, and so developing his wants. Wants, however, had to be guided prudently, for they could turn men toward the ale houses as well as the shops and factories. Most certain of all conditions leading them to industry was environment. If the poor could not be brought to gainful activity by monetary rewards or enticed to it by the desire to excel, they could be forced to it by necessity. Moreover, as Temple explained, the habits they formed while overcoming necessity would remain with them, and they would continue to be industrious when the original cause had disappeared.

III

In these observations on individual motivation, the mercantilist writers anticipated the economic psychology in classical doctrine. In addition, they anticipated two other of its important features: the nature of the price mechanism and the political presuppositions of economic policy.

It was the classical view that self-interest operating in a competitive market directed resources to their most efficient employments and enabled individuals to spend their income in a way which would maximize their satisfaction as consumers. Whatever interfered with the operation of self-interest, as it directed the choices of individuals in their capacity as producers or consumers, usually reduced the efficiency of the economy or, what is the same thing, its real income. The classicists did make exceptions to laissez faire, some of them insistent, but laissez faire was certainly their rule of policy. So great was their emphasis on the efficiency of resource use which the market created that one must suppose they believed the market would provide for the full employment of resources as well as their direction to the best particular uses. Apart from Malthus and Sismondi, none of the classicists admitted a conflict between efficient employment and full employment.

The mercantilists' conception of the price mechanism was similar to that of the classicists on these matters: the directive power of self-interest (that is, its economic as well as psychological aspect); the determination of prices by supply and demand; the desirability of competition; and the mutual advantage of exchange in domestic markets. The mercantilists, however, did not believe that universal efficiency could be established by the price system; they did believe that a limited operation of the system was desirable. They also held a qualified notion of the harmony of self-interest. On the issue of full employment, there was the greatest difference between the mercantilists and the classical economists. It was the mercantilist view that free international trade would reduce employment, that inattention to the monetary system would

have the same result, and that a highly unequal distribution of income could reduce spending which in turn would reduce employment. . . .

Hence, instead of the classical policy of laissez faire, the mercantilists proposed a policy which would utilize the market wherever possible, supplement and control it where not, and which would have full employment as its proximate objective. There was, then, this difference of *means* between the mercantilists and the classicists: the former proposed a relatively controlled market and the latter a relatively uncontrolled one. There also was a difference in emphasis on proximate *ends*: the mercantilists stressed the full employment of resources and the classicists stressed the efficiency of the use of particular resources.

Yet it will not do to carry these differences much farther. The difference about means was not a fundamental one. The mercantilists did not believe in an economy wholly or mainly directed by the state, and the classicists did not believe in an economy entirely controlled by a competitive market. The difference about means was a difference over the amount and kinds of control. Both classicists and mercantilists believed in what we now call a mixed economy, and they differed over the ingredients in the mixture. This kind of difference, we know today, is singularly hard to define and to resolve.

The difference on immediate ends — full employment versus efficiency of employment — also is one which must not be made fundamental. It is very probable that neither the mercantilists nor the classicists would have admitted such a distinction. The former, I suspect, would have insisted that their policy achieved a greater output, and therefore more efficiency, than a policy which ignored the problem of full employment. Their implicit assumption was that a nation was set free to choose between using *all* of its resources in one way or another, in order to satisfy the criterion of maximum output, but that the nation must choose between a policy which would produce full employment and one which would not. The classicists probably would have insisted that once the market had been made competitive and the conditions established for an efficient use of resources there would be no problem of full employment. They would have granted, perhaps insisted, that unwise interference with the market could create underemployment but they would not have admitted underemployment as a problem once the market was properly organized. It is only a later age which can make the distinction between full employment and efficient employment a certain one; and in order to do this it must define each of these objectives differently from the way they were defined by the mercantilists and the classicists. It must assume that a policy which provides full employment probably would be accompanied by some inefficiency in the use of particular resources, and that a policy which yields efficiency in the use of employed resources would be accompanied by a condition of some idle labor and capital. When the objectives are so defined, a choice can be made between the two policies, and that will be chosen which yields the largest national product. No clear choice is, however, implied by the distinction between the mercantilist and the classical policies. Not only is it unnecessary to speculate over which was correct, but, it seems to me, the speculation is a little pointless.

IV

It is more promising to speculate over the reasons for the difference between the mercantilist and the liberal objectives. The most plausible reason is that the two policies were developed in different periods in which there were different economic problems. The great concern of the mercantilists over employment, particularly of labor, may have been forced on them by the unemployment of the sixteenth, seventeenth, and early eighteenth centuries, which, economic historians tell us, and we can infer from contemporary tracts, was considerable. The enclosure movement seems to have

been the major cause of unemployment in the first part of the mercantilist period. By replacing tillage with grazing, the enclosures reduced the amount of labor required in agriculture and drove large numbers of persons off the land into rural slums and into the towns and cities. The transfer of large numbers from one occupation to another is difficult even under favorable circumstances; and circumstances in the sixteenth century were not favorable. The crafts guilds were not eager to increase their output at any time, and one can easily suppose that they were not pleased by the hordes who were swept off the land and sought employment in the towns.

Another cause of unemployment was the frequent commercial crises which by their strangeness must have baffled the early economists (no less than the later). Although the fluctuations seem not to have been of regular occurrence, as later cyclical movements were, yet these were more than occasional and sporadic changes. In addition to these two types of unemployment, which today would be called frictional and cyclical, there seems also to have been much seasonal unemployment. Petty's statistics on annual and weekly wages in the third quarter of the seventeenth century suggest that the average worker was employed about thirty-five weeks of the year.

It is fairly clear that unemployment was extensive and quite clear that poverty was common. The management of these two problems was made more than usually difficult by a circumstance arising from the Reformation. When the power of the Catholic church was destroyed there went with it an organized method of caring for the poor. An effort was made to place the responsibility on local governments, but this was not successful. The craft guilds, it is true, looked out for their members, but were unable to care for the newly created poor from agriculture even if they had wished to.

Not only was there less provision for the lower classes, but after the middle of the seventeenth century there was less interest in their welfare and less concern over the problem of unemployment. Under the Tudors there seems to have been a genuine solicitude for the lower classes, a feeling which perhaps came of the knowledge that disaffection with an absolute monarch can have disastrous results. After the revolution of 1688, the monarchy was severely abridged and therefore was less responsible for the general welfare, while Parliament could be only a diffuse object of resentment to those who thought the state was not looking after them properly. Elizabeth could say with reason, "Yet this I account the glory of my crown, that I have reigned with your loves." It is difficult to imagine words of the same sincerity coming from a sovereign after 1688.

It seems, to use today's language, that the unemployment of the sixteenth and seventeenth centuries was the result of immobility, of seasonal fluctuations, of the rigidity of certain prices and wages which was produced by the monopolistic practices of the guilds, and of frequent and severe deflations. The nonseasonal unemployment might have been eliminated (it now is easy to say) had it been possible to move labor from areas where it was abundant to where it was scarce and to force a reduction of certain wages and prices in order to make increased employment profitable to the entrepreneurs of the age. But it does not seem, from their writings, that the mercantilists thought such measures would have been adequate. Although they made proposals for increasing labor mobility and for making wages and prices more flexible, they do not seem to have put much reliance on them. Instead, it seems they had greater confidence in inflationary measures: those which, by increasing the money supply, would have increased spending and employment.

It is interesting to observe that Great Britain had a similar unemployment problem about 200 years after the close of the mercantilist period and solved it by methods quite suggestive of the mercantilists' proposals. After the first World War there

was considerable frictional unemployment and money wages could not easily have been lowered. A few years after the second World War, after the inflationary measures of the Labor Government had shown their effect, it was observed by a United Nations report on economic stability, that the frictional unemployment "which had previously been attributed mainly to lack of mobility of labour, melted away, leaving an acute labour shortage." This report was written mainly from the viewpoint of Keynesian economics which, it is clear, has an affinity to mercantilist doctrine.

In the period when liberal economic doctrine developed circumstances were much different from those of the mercantilist period. There was no longer the problem of managing a large amount of permanent unemployment, as this effect of the enclosure movement had disappeared. The internal market of Great Britain was much better organized, in the sense of there being less immobility of commodities and capital as well as of labor. By 1750, the government no longer enforced any important controls over the internal market. The obstacles to price and wage flexibility were much less formidable than they had been in the preceding three centuries. Improvements in transportation, especially after 1800, brought the parts of the economy into closer connection and made competition more feasible. Finally, there was an expansion of British foreign trade, resulting from the decline of the Dutch empire at the end of the seventeenth century, from the weakening of the imperial power of Spain, and from the increased efficiency of manufactures and shipping which gave Britain a cost advantage in the world market. These circumstances dictated a much wider use of the market as the appropriate economic policy, just as the different circumstances confronting the mercantilists required restrictions on the market. . . .

v

The interpretation of this essay makes English mercantilist doctrine a predecessor of economic liberalism. In order that the meaning be clear, it may be helpful to compare it to other interpretations of mercantilism. It is common for works on the history of economic thought to abide by the judgment of Smith and Mill, that the mercantilists believed money was wealth and therefore believed the nation became richer as its supply of monetary metal increased. It is understandable that the mercantilists should be judged this way. If their goal of full employment is neglected, there is no way to explain their preoccupation with the money supply but to suppose they thought money was wealth. The exposition above of their monetary theory should make clear that few of them made the simple error of which they have so often been accused.

Another interpretation looks upon mercantilist doctrine as a collection of mistaken ideas, not only in the area of monetary theory but in other areas as well. The mercantilists, by this view, are regarded as rudimentary economists who sensed the importance of the problems they addressed but were defeated by them. The mercantilists did express certain ideas crudely and they made mistakes (which is not at all singular). But there was nothing primitive about their central ideas. The most important aspects of the price mechanism, for example, were understood as long ago as 1549 when Hales's *Discourse* was published, and the way in which he wrote of them suggests they were known even earlier. Modern economics has expressed these principles more rigorously but it has not altered them. We still believe that unequal rates of profit will cause a re-allocation of transferable resources. Indeed, it is only in recent years that economics has tried to reintegrate monetary and price theory, in order to bring together the money and the real sides of the economy, which is a theoretical achievement sought by the mercantilists.

A third interpretation makes the mercantilists into apologists for the kind of economy in which they lived. It has become increasingly common in recent years to look upon social thought as an apology or rationalization of the social institutions which are dominant when the thought is expressed. When the mercantilists are regarded this way, two conclusions usually result. One is that their doctrine was an effort to explain the circumstances of their age. If this means the mercantilists were interested only in their period, it is wholly — and trivially — correct. Economists always are interested in the problems of the time, some of which are transitory and others nearly everlasting. The other conclusion is that the mercantilists sought to advance private interests by disguising them in a tissue of abstraction. I do not know how such an interpretation can be upheld (in addition to contrary statements in their works, there is the awkward difficulty of uncovering the private thoughts of men who have been dead 200 years and more), nor do I see just what significance the proof would have. Perhaps John Hales was trying to increase the income of corn growers and Thomas Mun wanted greater dividends for the East India Company. Nevertheless, they had something of lasting interest to say. . . .

The most cogent of all interpretations makes mercantilism a continuation of the ideas of medieval society. This is the view of Schmoller and of Heckscher. Schmoller stated that the principal tenet of mercantilism was the identity between political and economic institutions, such that the economic conduct of the individual was made to conform to the objectives of the state. Mercantilism was thus a system of national power and one of a number of forms which idealism as a political philosophy can take. Prior to the twentieth century dictatorships, the most notable expression of idealism was medieval society. In their remarks on economic conduct, the Schoolmen stated that free individual behavior was inimical to the welfare of society. They adopted the Aristotelean idea that exchange was "unnatural" because it caused men to lose sight of the proper use of commodities, which was consumption, and to make an improper use of them, which was unlimited accumulation.

In the Aristotelean and medieval conception, exchange is condemned if its purpose is anything more than the satisfaction of limited wants. It is wrong if it becomes a means of expressing acquisitive desires because these in themselves are improper. In its practical aspect, the conception makes exchange a useless, or barren, act, and imposes numerous controls over it. This was the medieval view after about the twelfth century, although there were exceptions to it.

In English mercantilist writings I have found only one statement which in any way suggests the medieval notion of exchange. It is Cary's assertion that the buying and selling "whereby one man lives by the profit of another, brings no advantage to the public." However, it is not certain that Cary endorsed the medieval idea. His observations on the price mechanism are anything but medieval. Admittedly, the mercantilists stated that self-interest was inimical to the public good, but the statement is, I believe, of no significance. The kind of economy they proposed could not possibly have operated without the expression of self-interest, just as the economy proposed by the classicists could not have operated without it. They too condemned self-interest, but neither they nor the mercantilists believed it wholly bad or even mainly so, and they did not want it suppressed. Both wanted the power it gave to men to be used in the national interest. Hales wrote:

> To tell you plainly, it is avarice that I take for the principal cause thereof [of enclosures]; but can we devise that all covetousness may be taken from men? No, no more than we can make men to be without ire, without gladness, without fear, and without all affections. What then? We must take away from men the occasion of their covetousness in this part. What is that? The exceeding lucre that they see grow by these enclosures, more than by husbandry. And that may be done by any of these two means that I will tell you: either by minishing the lucre that men have by grazing; or else by advancing of the profit of husbandry, till it be as good and as profitable to the occupiers as grazing is.

To exploit the selfishness in men, to reward them for it, to see in it a power for good as well as harm, were ideas as remote from the ruling thought of the Middle Ages as ideas could be. It is quite impossible there to discover the roots of English mercantilist doctrine. They took hold after the power of medievalism in England had passed. The direction of the doctrine laid not to the past but to the future, to the ideas of the classical economists, however much they disdained their predecessors. It is ironic that the doctrine should have been disparaged most by the men whose ideas it anticipated and that it should have been pushed back into an age with which it could have nothing in common.

Scholasticism and Mercantilism

RAYMOND DE ROOVER

Raymond Adrien de Roover (born 1904), after graduating from the Institut Superieur de Commerce in Antwerp in 1924, became an accountant in the Belgian shipping line the Agence Maritime Internationale. Later he studied at Harvard and Chicago. He is the author of a large number of books and articles dealing with the history of money and banking in the middle ages and the early modern period. Among them are *The Medici Bank, Its Organization, Management, Operations and Decline* (1948), *Money, Banking and Credit in Medieval Bruges* (1948), and *Gresham on Foreign Exchange* (Cambridge, Mass., 1949).

Raymond de Roover is presently professor of economics at Brooklyn College, New York.

THE DIFFERENCES between mercantilism and scholastic economics are striking and profound. Yet, I do not know that a comparison has ever been attempted, although a clear perception of the contrasts has its importance for an understanding of the development of economic thought. There are even historians who profess to find the "prehistory" of economics among the vagaries of the mercantilistic pamphleteers, thus completely ignoring the contributions of the Doctors.

Unlike mercantilism, scholastic economics enjoyed the unquestioned superiority of being an integral part of a coherent philosophical system. Although economics was not yet acknowledged as an independent discipline, it formed a consistent body of doctrine according to which economic relations ought to be ruled by the laws of distributive and commutative justice. In contrast, mercantilism was never more than a conglomerate of unco-ordinated prescriptions by which the authors of the mercantilistic tracts sought to influence economic policy, usually in a sense favorable to their private interests.

The Doctors, as this name indicates, were all university graduates, trained in theology or in canon and civil law (*doctor utriusque juris*). Most of them were clerics, though there are some notable exceptions among the jurists, especially among the civilians, for instance, Messer Lorenzo di Antonio Ridolfi, who was a layman, a diplomat and a lecturer at the Florentine athenaeum. The mercantilists, on the contrary, were with few exceptions self-trained merchants, with some literary talents, but without university degrees. Essentially, they were empiricists who, for better or for worse, were not encumbered by scholastic traditions. In this way they made their major contribution by developing the balance-of-trade theory, whereas the Doctors were unable to cut themselves loose from their traditional approach to the foreign exchange problem.

As a rule, the mercantilist writings were brief tracts on specific and controversial issues, which contrast markedly with the weighty and often pedantic treatises of the Doctors. Whereas the mercantilist pamphlets rarely refer to sources or provide

Reprinted by permission of the publishers from Raymond de Roover, "Scholastic Economics: Survival and Lasting Influence from the Sixteenth Century to Adam Smith: Scholasticism and Mercantilism; A Contrast," *The Quarterly Journal of Economics*, LXIX (1955), 177–85. Cambridge, Mass.: Harvard University Press, Copyright, 1955, by the President and Fellows of Harvard College.

marginal notes, the scholastic treatises literally bristle with references in support of nearly every statement, even the most commonplace. This sometimes annoying display of erudition, first introduced by the post-glossators, received further encouragement from the humanists, who developed the habit of invoking the authority of the Ancients for everything.

By the very fact that the Doctors were moralists, their main preoccupation was with social justice and general welfare, but naturally with these ideals as they were conceived in the Middle Ages and the sixteenth and seventeenth centuries. The mercantilists, too, professed to further the cause of the commonweal; however, their declarations in this respect should not always be taken at their face value. All too often they serve as a screen for private interests. Most of the authors of mercantilist tracts had an ax to grind. This is especially true of the early mercantilists. Gérard de Malynes (fl. 1586–1641) was a perennial office-seeker who advocated exchange control in the hope that he himself would be appointed the controller. Misselden (fl. 1608–1654) and John Wheeler (fl. 1601–1608) were spokesmen for the Merchant Adventurers; and Thomas Mun (1571–1641) wrote his tracts in defense of the East India Company. As for Gresham (1519–1579), he was a shrewd and none too scrupulous manipulator of the money market, whose recommendations, although advantageous to the Queen, were apt to have unfavorable repercussions on English trade and on the volume of employment. The later mercantilists were less prejudiced, but their views were still warped by their narrow nationalism. Most of them rallied to the defense of the colonial system and sponsored aggressive measures to combat or to exclude foreign competition, an attitude which is alien to the spirit of scholasticism. Did not St. Thomas justify international trade by pointing out the fact that no nation is self-sufficient?

[But] the casuists of the seventeenth century were either unwilling or unable to rejuvenate their methods. They continued in the old ruts and made no effort to incorporate new discoveries, such as the balance-of-trade theory, into their traditional doctrines. The conservatism of the late scholastic writers thus became an impediment to further progress, and it is fortunate that the mercantilists displayed more initiative and did not hesitate to blaze new trails. True, their methods were not always sound, nor always successful, but they opened up new avenues for further research. The controversy of the early mercantilists about exchange control led to a premature proposal for the creation of a stabilization fund and eventually culminated in the formulation by Thomas Mun of the balance-of-trade theory. The mercantilists also made the first clumsy attempts to use statistical data, and Sir William Petty (1623–1687) even made statistics the basis of his *Political Arithmetick*. Others pondered over banking schemes; and the studies of Charles Davenant (1656–1714) and Gregory King (1648–1712) on the behavior of grain prices put them on the track of the elasticity of demand. The seventeenth century was the age of projectors. Nearly always, the aim was to influence public policy, whereas the scholastic writers were content to set up ethical standards, but left their practical realization to the often inefficient government authorities.

The scholastic writers regarded trade as an occupation which, although not evil in itself, endangered the salvation of the soul, as the merchants almost unavoidably succumbed to the temptations of usury, cheating, and unlawful gain: *et de hoc rarissime evadunt mercatores*, as St. Bonaventure (1221–1275), the Seraphic Doctor, testifies. In this opinion, the other Doctors concur: without exception, they much prefer agriculture to trade. The mercantilist writers, of course, take exactly the opposite point of view. In their eyes trade is the noblest of all professions. Both agriculture and industry depend on trade to provide a market for their products and to give employment to the "poor." The merchant, far from being regarded with distrust, is extolled as the benefactor of humanity and the principal pillar of the State. This is what one might expect, since mercantilism was the economic system developed by, and for, the merchants.

In contrast to scholastic economics, mercantilism was amoral. The later mercantilists were interested in a large population and full employment only because they thought such conditions would stimulate trade and increase the economic power of the state. Usury was no longer considered a voracious monster: Sir Josiah Child (1630–1699), Sir Thomas Culpeper the Elder, and others complained only that the interest rate, being higher in England than in Holland, favored the competition of the Dutch. Trade has no soul and the individual did not count: why should the mercantilists be disturbed by moral issues?

One of the most striking characteristics of scholastic economics was universalism: regardless of origin and nationality, the Doctors are in fundamental agreement on method and principles. Although there may be, sometimes, sharp differences on points of detail or of practical application, all their treatises follow more or less the same pattern easily recognizable by anyone acquainted with scholastic literature. In the mercantilist camp, on the contrary, such uniformity in doctrine or method does not exist: neither between national schools nor between individual writers.

Among the mercantilists, "everyone is his own economist," according to the phrase so aptly coined by Professor E. A. J. Johnson. No one considers himself bound by precedent, and each author follows his own inspiration in selecting the appropriate method for dealing with his chosen topic. Notwithstanding the great prestige of Eli F. Heckscher, I disagree with his statement that mercantilism strove toward unity. As a matter of fact, non-scholastic economics in the seventeenth and eighteenth centuries varied greatly from country to country. In my opinion, the name "mercantilism" is appropriate only for British eco-

nomics during that period. In Germany, one should speak of cameralism. One of its leading exponents, Johann Joachim Becher (1635–1682), "was still strongly influenced by the venerable Aristotelian tradition," albeit that he considerably modified the scholastic views. In France, the expression "Colbertism," rather than "mercantilism," should be used to designate the economic policy of Colbert. Moreover, this policy aroused much criticism from writers such as Vauban (1633–1707) and his cousin Boisguilbert (1646–1714), whose comments on the iniquities of the French tax system anticipated the physiocrats instead of doing something to mercantilist ideas.

Although the United Provinces were the leading economic power in the seventeenth century, there exists as yet no adequate study on Dutch economic thought during this period. At any rate, Hugo Grotius or de Groot deserves a niche in the gallery of famous economists. One can hardly classify him as a mercantilist; he was rather an Aristotelian who used scholastic methods to defeat scholasticism. Even Pieter de la Court (1618–1685), although not an Aristotelian, is far too liberal to pass for a mercantilist.

In Spain, after 1600, economic writers, without breaking with scholasticism, were mainly concerned with the country's ailments: vellon inflation, vagrancy, depopulation, and economic decline. Whether this concern with pressing social and economic problems labels them as mercantilists remains a debatable point. As in Spain, so also in Italy the scholastic traditions were particularly strong, and persisted well into the eighteenth century along with other currents of thought originating in the merchant manuals of the Middle Ages. In 1613, a Neapolitan writer, Dr. Antonio Serra, in fighting a scheme to regulate foreign exchange, formulated independently the balance-of-trade theory developed contemporaneously by the English mercantilists. His proposals were dismissed, and his book was ignored for more than a century until abbé Ferdinando Galiani praised it as an outstanding performance. The witty abbé expresses his surprise that a book like Serra's was conceived "in an age of ignorance about economic matters," but he complains that the work is "tedious" reading because of its obscure style, its poor organization, and its "divisions and subdivisions" reminiscent of scholastic literature. In other words, the abbé is a typical example of the eighteenth-century point of view. Another interesting fact is that Galiani considers the work of Serra to be scholastic, whereas most modern authors have classed it as a mercantilist pamphlet.

The trouble is that the word "mercantilism" does not stand for a clear concept, but lends itself to confusion. The great specialist Heckscher, himself, has to admit that "mercantilism is simply a convenient term for summarizing a phase of economic policy and economic ideas." It should be added that the term covers only those heterogeneous ideas that are non-scholastic in inspiration.

There are remnants of scholastic influence in many mercantilist writings, but surprisingly those traces have not been recognized, though they are not so difficult to spot. The mercantilists, of course, were unable to escape from the impact of several centuries of culture. Whether or not they knew it, they absorbed some of the ideas bequeathed by former generations.

. . . The mercantilists have been praised [by William Grampp] for the "liberalism" of their concepts. Contrary to the conclusions of the author, it appears, however, that those so-called "liberal elements" are rooted in the doctrines of the medieval Schoolmen. For one thing, the Doctors were uncompromising in their condemnation of monopoly for the reason that the monopolist exploits the public and makes an illicit gain by raising the price of his articles above the competitive level. For

example, Cardinal Cajetan, commenting on the *Summa* of Thomas Aquinas states that monopoly offends freedom by compelling the public to pay a price higher than the one that would prevail in the market, if there were no such monopoly (*si huiusmodi monopolium non esset*). The traditional feeling against monopoly was so strong that no mercantilist writer dared openly defy public opinion, even when his purpose was to justify the monopolistic practices of this or that trading company. In the parlance of the mercantilists, "free trade," . . . meant freedom from restraints of any sort in internal as well as in foreign trade. Consequently, it corresponded to the French expression *liberté du commerce* and not to *libre échange*. In the seventeenth century, protection in the modern sense was not yet born; the struggle was still a medieval struggle for the control of the carrying trade. In dealing with the history of economic thought, it is not enough to know the writings of the economists; one must also know something about the institutional framework and the social environment of the period.

Certainly, the English "mercantilists did not believe in an economy wholly or mainly directed by the State," but they wanted the state to pursue a policy favorable to the trading interests and they tended to defend the exclusive privileges of chartered companies and corporations. Owing to the persistent influence of scholastic ideals, the mercantilists paid lip service to the goddess of "free trade," though the sincerity of their devotion is very much open to question, inasmuch as their pretenses conflict with other aims. But then, mercantilism was not a logical system. It may even plausibly be argued that, unlike scholasticism, the much vaunted mercantile system was not a system at all.

Social Mercantilism

CHARLES WILSON

Charles Wilson (born 1914) is a fellow of Jesus College, Cambridge, England, and professor of modern history in the University of Cambridge since 1963. He has a specialist interest in the economic history of England in the seventeenth and eighteenth centuries, as his books show: *Anglo-Dutch Commerce and Finance in the Eighteenth Century* (Cambridge, 1941), *Profit and Power, a Study of England and the Dutch Wars* (London, 1957), and *England's Apprenticeship, 1603–1763* (London, 1965). With his two-volume *History of Unilever* he has also made a substantial contribution to business history. Since the war he has been one of the main commentators on mercantilism, as his writings demonstrate. In this article he turns aside from the previous debate to a discussion of the nature of social policy in England between 1660 and 1760.

I N ENGLAND," Sir John Seeley once wrote, "it is our custom to alter things but to leave their names unaltered." Anyone who wished to test the truth of the dictum historiographically might examine the history of the word "mercantilism." It has borne many, sometimes oddly conflicting, meanings, but they have had at any rate one thing in common: they have all been in some degree unpalatable to those reared in the traditions of English liberal thought. It was the conspiracy of a mercantile minority out to line its pockets at the expense of the rest of the community that the system was first depicted by the classical economists. . . .

The picture that has been created is that of a ruthlessly materialistic ruling class which did not merely neglect but actively exploited the poor. "Mercantilists," an authority on economic thought writes, "if they held any wage theory at all, believed in an economy of low wages." For Miss Margaret James the social legislators of the Restoration "aimed at nothing less than making the poor a source of profit to the state by forcing them to work for reduced wages." The presence of a few nobly philanthropic exceptions to this general rule was not enough to soften the indictment. Firmin, the London mercer of Socinian leanings, who experimented in social reform or the Quaker, Bellers, whose *Proposals for a College of Industry* (1695) showed deep concern for social welfare, emerge as entirely exceptional figures, quite untypical of their age. How far is all this a just and representative account of the aims and attitudes of the governing classes of Britain in the years that followed the Restoration?

*   *   *

Historians have underestimated the gravity and oversimplified the complexity of the great debate of the poor. Faced by the difficulty of analysing the relation between states of mind and private interests, between thoughts and actions, they have too often been satisfied with what are fundamentally *a priori* conclusions. It is now apparent that between the Restoration and (say) the end of the Seven Years' War England faced a chronic problem of poverty which affected severely somewhere between a quarter and a half of the whole population. It was not only the large num-

From Charles Wilson, "The Other Face of Mercantilism," *Transactions of the Royal Historical Society,* IX (1959), 81–101. By permission of the author and the Royal Historical Society.

ber of real paupers but the high proportion of casual part-time workers in the nation's leading industry, clothmaking, that
constituted the problem. Gregory King's
Tables included a figure of over a million
and a quarter for "cottagers, paupers, va-
grants, gypsies, thieves, beggars" out of a
total of five and a half million in 1688.
Population growth and industrial change
had faced seventeenth-century England
with a social problem that the Middle Ages
had never known: an army of workers
partly or wholly dependent on a great but
unstable manufacturing export industry.
One of the motives behind the mercantilist
urge to diversify the nation's industries had
been the consciousness that fluctuations in
the demand for cloth might (as Mun put
it) "suddenly cause much poverty and dangerous uproars, specially by our poor people." Politics and Nature had combined to
endorse his warning. At home and abroad
wars had continually disrupted markets
and it is at least arguable that at two points
— 1652 and 1665 — the decision to fight the
Dutch may have been influenced by the
belief that the trade depression might
thereby be relieved. Vigorous industries in
Holland and France were now competing
for Europe's shrunken cloth markets and
Colbert had placed the forces of the state
in the balance. By the end of the century,
the structure of the industry was adjusting
itself to the stresses of the times. The less
competitive areas of the West Country
were yielding ground to East Anglia, as
both these areas were in the eighteenth
century to yield to the Yorkshire industry.
On an industrial pattern already distorted
by human violence must be superimposed
the effects of the disastrous harvests which
supervened from time to time. 1649, for
example, a year of regicide, mutiny, dis-
order and upheaval, was also visited by an
appalling harvest that drove up grain prices
to famine heights and added to the grievous
trade depression. On top of the French
wars of the '90's came especially bad harvests in 1692, 1693, 1695, 1698, 1708 and
1709. The severity of the hardship created

by these conjunctions of normal and exceptional stresses undoubtedly helped to de-
flect the course of economic thought.

*   *   *

The profusion of welfare economics of
1649 seems to me to form the basis of almost all later economic thought for more
than a century. The recognition that the
problem of poverty, employment and national welfare are all linked together was
never subsequently lost sight of. It was to
appear again whenever bad times provoked
men to brood on social remedies. 1659, a
bad year, brought forth Cornelius Plockhoy's *A Way Propounded to Make the
Poor in This and Other Nations Happy*.
Between then and the crisis of the '90's
writers like Child, Matthew Hale, Robert
Harford, Firmin, Davenant, Yarranton,
Locke and others developed the theme.
The debate was resumed at full length between 1692 and 1709 with the new editions of Child's *Discourse*. John Bellers
published his *Proposals for a College of
Industry* in 1695, and two years later his
*Epistle to Friends Concerning the Educa-
tion of Children*. There is a strong general
resemblance between these and other writings of the '90's — Dudley North's *Discourses* (1691), *Britannia Languens* (1696)
and John Cary's *Essay* (1696).

Some might support and others oppose
the idea of parish factories, as Defoe opposed Sir Humphrey Mackworth's Bill for
those institutions in 1724, but one idea had
come to be firmly established in the popular mind: the potential value of the labour
represented by the nation's poor. Nor can
the general approach to the problem be dismissed as merely cynical or self-interested.
It had become too plain that poverty was
the dominant social problem. Post-Restora-
tion mercantilists were no longer so ab-
sorbedly preoccupied, as their predecessors
had been, with state welfare measured in
the narrow terms of the net amount of
bullion gained or lost via the balance of
trade. This traditional obsession was now
blended with a concern for the social needs

of the community which had its roots in the ideas of 1649. The obstinate core of mercantilist thought can nevertheless be seen in the belief that some activities were beneficial and some harmful to the community and that it was the State's task to discern and separate the two.

At this point I can imagine the critics moving to their second line of defence. "We may" (they might well say) "have omitted to count one or two heads, neglected one or two principles. But does this affect the argument? Does not the story remain one of neglect and harshness? Even granting that their motives were less blameworthy than has sometimes been supposed, did not deeds lag a long way behind intentions?" Certainly there is no lack of evidence to substantiate the gloomiest view of society in the hundred years under review. The originals of Tom Nero, Mother Needham, Tom Idle and the rest may all be discovered in the fearful annals of St. Giles, Shoreditch, Drury Lane and Alsatia. This last century before the Industrial Revolution is near enough the present to invite comparison of its social and moral standards with those of a later day. Even now that it is a commonplace to say that the civilization of the Augustan Age was but a veneer, it comes as something of a shock to read the Report of the Commons Committee on the Care of the Poor in the Parish of St. Martin-in-the-Fields in 1715. Three-quarters out of the twelve hundred babies born every year in the parish died, many being exposed or overlaid by "nurses." Money was stolen, accounts were falsified, paupers were starved and in some cases murdered. Consider the later inquiries of Jonas Hanway, Russia merchant and social reformer, founder of the Marine Society, the Magdalen House and the Foundling Hospital, and one of the most indefatigable and splendid bores of English history. His seventy-four separate works on charitable problems seem, again, to underline the failure of private enterprise to find any solution to the social problem. In the fourteen parishes investigated by him he calculated that the death-rate amongst infants entering or being born in the workhouses that had sprung up since 1720 was 88%. Some parishes (it was said) acknowledged that "no infant had lived to be apprenticed from their workhouses." Under the system by which the poor were hired out to a contractor, the workhouse had become a place of vice, a catchall for the infant and the infirm, the able-bodied idle and the criminal alike. Some of this may have been exaggerated but much was undoubtedly true. Is the true explanation to be found (as some historians have suggested) in a decline of charity, in a harsher and more censorious attitude toward povery and misfortune? The title of Professor Tawney's chapter on this period — "The New Medicine for Poverty" — gives a suitably sinister twist to the theme. Statistical comparisons of virtue, whether of individuals or societies, are not a promising branch of historical inquiry. But there exists one source of information as to the extent, if not the quality, of charity in England which has not (so far as I am aware) been analysed. Under the provisions of Gilbert's Act of 1782, the Ministers and Church-wardens of the parishes of England and Wales were required to make a return of all the Charitable Trusts then existing, with the date of creation, the name of the donor, the object, the capital and annual income, and the title of the Trustees responsible for administering the charity. In all, some sixty or seventy thousand separate donations, mainly of seventeenth and eighteenth-century origin were recorded. They yielded a total annual income of £258,000 spread over all the counties of England and Wales. All but £6,236 came from English returns — a capital value all told of some £5 million in the ratio of £5 worth of land for every £1 of other types of investment. The majority of the benefactors defined their intentions only in general terms: food and clothing or fuel for the poor. A few were more specific. These poor were to have beef, those herrings; some got linen, others woollens. Poor men were to have coats, or shirts and shifts, poor women to have gowns. There was to be provision "to marry poor maidens." The poor here were to have Bibles, the poor children there to have books. This village was to have an almshouse, another a charity school. Mr. Tomkins of Abingdon would relieve "poor Dissenters (but not Papists)." And so on. Obscurities abound. Many charities have no date. Many no doubt were omitted. There are hints at misappropriation. Of many a benefaction the authorities could only observe: "but we do not apprehend that it was ever received."

*   *   *

Amongst the many uncertainties in the returns of charities one trend emerges clearly: the growing proportion of donors who felt moved to endow some form of active apprenticeship or instruction for the juvenile poor, as distinct from the passive forms of relief common in earlier periods. It is a reminder that these were the early years of that remarkable movement for charity schools which was co-ordinated from 1699 by the S.P.C.K. Hundreds of thousands of children, for whom no other means of education existed, received in the thousands of such schools the rudiments of education, religion and practical training that gave them a chance to earn a living. At the peak of the movement the boys went as apprentices into every kind of trade, the girls became sempstresses or domestic servants. Again, it is easy to put a cynical motive to the work, to point to the drift away from literary and religious studies to technical training and utility. Some falling away of standards there may have been. Yet the Charity Schools remain a notable instance of that principle of voluntary association which historians like Unwin and Tawney have rightly enjoined on us to behold and admire as a vital element in social development. No previous age had faced such a formidable social problem and none certainly had attempted to relieve, employ or educate an army of poor already alarmingly enlarged by natural increase. These improvisations in social service failed

or fell short of their object not because of a shortage of good intentions or of money, but because the supply of those capable of organizing and administering them with reasonable efficiency, honesty and compassionate understanding was totally inadequate. To read the replies made by parish governors to Hanway is to realize how appalling were the difficulties encountered in the organization of poor relief, how rarely a parish could find a treasure like the splendid Nurse Howe of St. Mary Whitechapel, how few were the Humphrey Clinkers, how numerous the Tom Neros. To endure the continual proximity of the poor a man needed to be either especially saintly or especially impervious to human suffering, cruelty, filth and corruption. In such a situation it was not unnatural that men should lose faith in the efficacy of high principles and take refuge in the reflection that "whate'er is best administered is best." Yet the art of administration was equally elusive. Administration, as the modern world understands it, is a Victorian invention resting on Victorian values: it ran counter to much that was characteristic of eighteenth-century society. Enough of the bad old days remained in 1857 to provide Charles Dickens with material for his classic satire on bureaucracy: the Circumlocution Office in *Little Dorrit*. He would not have been entirely at a loss for material a century later.

The apathy, indifference and chaos of the eighteenth-century poor law was the product not of a new capitalist ethic, but of the frustration, failure and occasional panic of a generation faced by a problem beyond its power to control. The heart of the matter was contained in the title of Defoe's famous pamphlet: *Everybody's Business is Nobody's Business* (1728). This applied not only to the condition of the institutions, but to the Settlement Laws themselves. Few historians today accept Adam Smith's famous strictures in the Laws at their face value, but it was a fact that they gave local authorities powers of ejectment that at first might appear ruthless. Yet here again, the preamble to the Act which explains why the powers were deemed necessary puts the problem in a different light. The provision of relief for the unemployed differed greatly between one parish and another and those parishes "which endeavoured to do their duty in this respect were inundated by distressed paupers." In short, what came to be regarded by later critics as a system of calculated brutality and repression arose in the first place not from unconcern or harshness, but out of a desire to protect the efforts of those local authorities who were trying hardest to improvise remedies.

Those who do not trust interventionism are apt to inveigh alternately against its wickedness and its futility. It cannot have been both. The influence of "policy" on the labour situation in the seventeenth century may have been exaggerated; certainly "policy" was to an important extent a reflection of social facts. Yet it seems an oddly misplaced modesty in scholars to disown the historical importance of ideas. The great Debate of the Poor conducted in Press, pamphlet and Parliament had helped to elucidate the importance of labour — skilled labour in particular — to the community. The facts of unemployment and poverty had joined with the ideas of educational reform that stemmed originally from Comenius and Milton and the junction stimulated a new emphasis on apprenticeship, training and skill. Later theories of labour value have their roots in these years. Yet though the debaters had broadened and socialized their criteria of the nation's economic welfare, they remained mercantilists to a man. Hartlib, for all his precocious concern with technology, monetary substitutes and the like, was not free from the orthodox preoccupation with shipping and "dominion on the sea and thereby the strength and renown and flourishing estate of the nation." Defoe has sometimes been credited with precociously free trade views on the strength of the part he played in Harley's *Mercator,* but in fact his views remained conventionally mercantilist and

protectionist. Firmin was amongst the stoutest opponents of the import of French textiles. Mandeville, for all his scorn of bullionism, remained firmly anchored to the old principles, enjoining upon politicians that "above all, they'll keep a watchful Eye over the Balance of Trade in general and never suffer that all the Foreign Commodities together, that are imported in one year, shall exceed in value what of their own growth or manufacture is in the same exported to others." The principles of *Machtpolitik* had no more single minded disciple than Jonas Hanway, who dedicated one of his principal works to Anson, the victor of Finisterre. John Cary, the great Bristol merchant and philanthropist, exemplified perfectly the union of mercantilist principles with ideals of social reform. The theme of his famous *Essay* of 1695 was that some trades were profitable to the nation and should be encouraged; others were harmful and should be discouraged. In making its decisions between the two, government should be guided not so much by the net effects on the bullion flow as by the results in terms of manufacture and employment. As an economist, Cary was heir to the ideas of Child — balance-of-trade-mercantilism modified by considerations of employment. His influence was exercised equally on trade policy and on social reform. But it was not only in England where his writings were widely distributed and read down to the mid-eighteenth century. This type of mercantilism — what might not unfairly be called "social mercantilism" — was the most powerful formative influence on continental mercantilism in the eighteenth century. Two of the founding Fathers of German *Kameralwissenschaft* — Becher and von Schroeder — were resident in England in these years (J. J. Becher fled to England in 1680 and remained here till his death in 1685; von Schroeder lived in London from about 1663 to 1674, when he returned to Germany) and the resemblance between the "equilibrium of occupation" of Schroeder's *Fürstliche Schatz und Rentkammer* (1686) and the ideas of Child and Cary is too close to be accidental. From this, three-quarters of a century later, came Sonnenfels's theory of the two trade balances by which economic health must be judged: the "monetary" and the "employment" balance. The genealogy of mercantilism in Italy is equally clear. When Genovesi came to establish a flourishing school of economics at Naples in the 1750's, he began by translating John Cary's *Essay* for his pupils' benefit, while relegating Mun's earlier work to an appendix. His own doctrine that distinguished between the "useful commerce" which exported manufactures and the "harmful" which brought in foreign manufactures, was the word precisely as Cary had preached it. There can be little doubt that the social and economic policy of Enlightened Despotism in Eastern Europe owed most of its theoretical foundations to English "social mercantilism." Even in France, the new synthesis was not without influence. De Gournay, then an *intendant* for commerce, who stood between the extremes of mercantilist and physiocratic dogma, published in 1754 a French edition of the works of Child and Culpeper. In some sense, England was only paying back an intellectual debt owed to Europe. For it is a remarkable fact that not a little of the "welfare" element in that doctrine may be traced to thinkers of European origin. Hartlib was a Pole, something of a cosmopolitan who spoke several languages including Dutch. Comenius, the source of much of the educational controversy of these years, was a Czech. Chamberlen was by origin French; Plockhoy, a Zeelander. Mandeville came from Rotterdam. That the debate which had begun round the theme of wealth and conquest had broadened into a debate on social ends was not a little due to their intervention. It was not only English economic and technological organization that was leavened by immigrant influence, but English social ideas, too.

SUGGESTIONS FOR ADDITIONAL READING

A brief but far-ranging pioneer account of the subject of mercantilism was provided by J. W. Horrocks, *A Short History of Mercantilism* (London, 1925), but the most detailed general discussion is to be found in the two volumes by Eli Heckscher entitled *Mercantilism* (London, 1935), of which a revised edition, which took scant notice of the criticism to which the first edition had been subjected, appeared in 1955. A shorter statement of Heckscher's view can be found in the article on "Mercantilism" in the *Encyclopedia of the Social Sciences* (New York, 1934–35). Leading the debate on Heckscher's view of mercantilism of recent years has been Charles Wilson, who is the author of a number of contributions on this subject. In 1958 he produced a pamphlet for the British Historical Association entitled *Mercantilism* which discussed the system in England and elsewhere, and the changing meaning attached to the word itself. This latter aspect was discussed in more detail in "Mercantilism: Some Vicissitudes of an Idea," *Economic History Review*, 2nd series, X (1957), 181–88. Wilson also contributed the section on the subject to the *Dictionary of the Social Sciences*, ed. J. Gould and W. L. Kolb (London, 1964). D. C. Coleman has also commented on Heckscher's views in "Eli Heckscher and the Idea of Mercantilism," *Scandinavian Economic History Review*, V (1957), 3–25. But Heckscher has not been without supporters. J. F. Rees wrote a historical revision of "Mercantilism," *History*, new series, XXIV (1939–40), 129–35, which was favorable to the concept, while A. W. Coats has written "In Defence of Heckscher and the Idea of Mercantalism," *Scandinavian Economic History Review*, V (1957), 173–87. More recent contributions are from Lars Herlitz, "The Concept of Mercantilisf," *Scandinavian Economic History Review*, XII (1964), 101–20, and Hermann Kellenbenz, "Probleme der Merkan-

tilismusforschung," XIIe Congrès Internationale des Sciences Historiques, *Rapports IV, Methodologie et histoire contemporaine*, 171–90.

More detailed discussion of mercantilism falls broadly under two heads: an account of the nature of mercantilist theory and an analysis of the characteristics of mercantilist policy. In the first respect the student who wishes to go further should pay some attention to the mercantilist writers themselves: In England, the writings of Thomas Mun (1571–1641), Josiah Child (1630–99), William Petty (1623–87), and Nicholas Barbon (1640?–98). Mun's *England's Treasure by Foreign Trade* is available in a modern reprint (Oxford, 1928 and 1949); pamphlets by Mun, Petty, and others are reprinted in J. R. McCulloch (ed.), *A Select Collection of Early English Tracts on Commerce* (1856: London, 1952). Child's "Brief Observations Concerning Trade, and Interest of Money" (1668) is reprinted in William Letwin, *Sir Josiah Child, Merchant Economist* (Boston, 1959). Passages from Mun and Petty are to be found in *Early Economic Thought: Selections from Economic Literature Prior to Adam Smith* (Cambridge, Mass., 1924), ed. A. E. Monroe, as well as extracts from the writings of Jean Bodin (1530–96), Antonio Serra, and Philipp Wilhelm von Hornigk (1638–1712).

The contribution of the mercantilists is assessed in many of the histories of economic thought. Among the best for our purpose are E. Roll, *A History of Economic Thought* (London, rev. ed., 1961); Alexander Gray, *The Development of Economic Doctrine* (London, 1931), and Mark Blaug, *Economic Theory in Retrospect* (London, 1964), but the most illuminating is Joseph A. Schumpeter, *A History of Economic Analysis* (New York, 1954). More detailed discussion of mercantilist thought can be found in E. A. J. Johnson, *Predecessors of Adam Smith, The Growth of*

British Economic Thought (New York, 1936, reprinted New York, 1960), which discusses ten writers separately and then deals with their theory of production; in M. Beer, *Early British Economics* (London, 1938); and W. Letwin, *The Origins of Scientific Economics* (New York, 1964), which concentrates on the writings of the English merchant economist, Sir Josiah Child.

Particular aspects of mercantilist theory have received especial treatment. The mercantilist view of the theory of international trade is considered by Jacob Viner in his *Studies in the Theory of International Trade* (New York, 1937) and by Br. Suviranta, *The Theory of the Balance of Trade in England; a Study in Mercantilism* (Helsingfors, 1923). A running debate on one aspect of this question, the importance of precious metals in the mercantilist scheme of things was carried on by Eli Heckscher and Charles Wilson, "Treasure and Trade Balances: The Mercantilist Problem," *Economic History Review*, 2nd series, II (1949), 152–61; E. Heckscher, "Multilateralism, Baltic Trade, and the Mercantilists," *Economic History Review*, 2nd series, III (1950), 219–28; and Charles Wilson, "Treasure and Trade Balances; Further Evidence," *Economic History Review*, 2nd series, IV (1951), 231–42. While Heckscher and Wilson based their argument largely on contemporary polemical literature, three further contributions relied on an analysis of customs records and of actual mercantile procedures: J. M. Price, "Multilateralism and/or Bilateralism: The Settlement of British Trade Balances with the 'North' c. 1700," *Economic History Review*, 2nd series, XIV (1961), 254–74, which argues that after 1660 with the silver shortage there was a greater use of the multilateral exchange mechanism; J. Sperling, "The International Payments Mechanism in the Seventeenth and Eighteenth Centuries," *Economic History Review*, 2nd series, XIV (1962), 446–68, which suggests that Wilson's arguments apply to the early seventeenth century and Heckscher's

to the later seventeenth and early eighteenth centuries; and Sven-Erik Aström, *From Cloth to Iron, The Anglo-Baltic Trade in the Late Seventeenth Century: Part I: The Growth, Structure and Organisation of the Trade* (Helsinki, 1963). Charles Wilson replied to this debate with "International Payments: An Interim Comment," *Economic History Review*, 2nd series, XV (1962), 364–69. See also J. H. Dales, "The Discoveries and Mercantilism: An Essay in History and Theory," *Canadian Journal of Economics and Political Science*, XXI (1955), 141–53, which constructs a model to illustrate the working of the trading system. The Heckscher-Wilson debate was concerned with the Baltic trade: the other leak of bullion was the trade with the Far East. For this see K. N. Chaudhuri, "The East India Company and the Export of Treasure in the Early Seventeenth Century," *Economic History Review*, 2nd series, XVI (1963), 23–38.

Other writers have considered further aspects: Joseph J. Spengler analyzes "Mercantilist and Physiocratic Growth Theory" in *Theories of Economic Growth*, ed. Bert Hoselitz (New York, 1960); Arthur E. Monroe deals with writings of the sixteenth, seventeenth, and early eighteenth centuries (as well as other writings) in *Monetary Theory before Adam Smith* (Cambridge, Mass., 1923); see also Douglas Vickers, *Studies in the Theory of Money, 1690–1776* (London, 1960). Harold B. Ehrlich considers "British Mercantilist Theories of Profit," *American Journal of Economics and Sociology*, XIV (1955), 377–86; and Philip Buck discusses *The Politics of Mercantilism* (New York, 1942; reprinted New York, 1964). Finally, for the place of war in mercantilist thought, see E. Silberner, *La Guerre et la paix dans l'histoire des doctrines economiques* (Paris, 1957).

Much of the scholarly discussion of mercantilism has drawn its inspiration rather from the deeds than the thought, from the practice rather than the theory. The best sources for the practice of mercantilism in general terms in Europe are Herbert Heaton, *Economic History of Europe* (New York, 1936 and later editions), which has useful bibliographical notes, and G. N. Clark, *The Seventeenth Century* (London, 2nd ed. 1947), Chapter III, "Economic Policy and Ideas."

Of the individual countries, the most voluminous literature concerns England. Practically all the writing on economic thought and policy in the sixteenth, seventeenth, and eighteenth centuries touches either directly or obliquely on mercantilist problems, so the ensuing list will do no more than indicate the more extensive reading. Patently influenced by Schmoller, Part I of W. Cunningham's *The Growth of English Industry and Commerce in Modern Times* (London, 5th ed., 1910–12) is entitled "The Mercantile System," and, within this volume, Section 3 is called "Parliamentary Colbertism." Similarly Volumes II and III of E. Lipson, *Economic History of England* (London, 4th ed., 1947) bear the title "The Age of Mercantilism." Lipson nailed his colors more firmly to the mast with his book on *A Planned Economy or Free Enterprise* (London, 2nd ed., 1946), in which he wrote of "England's First Planned Economy" in the sixteenth century. In similar vein is Conyers Read, "Mercantilism, the Old English Pattern of a Controlled Economy," which appeared in *The Constitution Reconsidered* (New York, 1938), edited by Conyers Read.

Again within English experience, attention has been focused on certain aspects of the subject — on the problem of labor, on questions of foreign trade and commercial policy, and on the role of the colonies. To the study of the problem of labor the most important contribution has been Edgar S. Furniss, *The Position of the Laborer in a System of Nationalism: A Study of the Labor Theories of the Later English Mercantilists* (Chicago, 1920, reprinted New York, 1957). See also T. E. Gregory, "The Economics of Employment in England, 1660–1715," *Economica*, I (1921), 37–51; and D. C. Coleman, "Labour in the English Economy of the 17th century," *Economic*

History Review, 2nd series, VIII (1956), 280–95, reprinted in E. Carus-Wilson, *Essays in Economic History*, II (London, 1962). M. G. Davies, *The Enforcement of English Apprenticeship: A Study in Applied Mercantilism 1563–1647* (Cambridge, Mass., 1956) is the most recent of a number of discussions of the working of this statute, but see also R. K. Kelsall, *Wage Regulations under the Statute of Artificers* (London, 1938). The origins of the act are discussed by S. T. Bindoff in "The Making of the Statute of Artificers" in *Elizabethan Government and Society*, ed. S. T. Bindoff, J. Hurstfield, and C. H. Williams (London, 1961).

In the course of many of the discussions of English foreign trade between 1500 and the middle of the eighteenth century, the question of mercantilist policy and its nature is overtly or covertly discussed. In his discussion of "Commercial Trends and Policy in 16th-Century England," *Economic History Review*, X (1940), 95–117, reprinted in E. M. Carus-Wilson, *Essays in Economic History*, I (London, 1954), 152–72, F. J. Fisher suggests that the Tudors were more forced than forceful. Raymond de Roover discussed the vexed question of the foreign exchanges in "What Is Dry Exchange? A Contribution to the Study of English Mercantilism," *Journal of Political Economy*, LII (1944), 250–66, and *Gresham and the Foreign Exchanges* (Cambridge, Mass., 1949).

Differences about the nature of the British commercial situation in the 1620's have given rise to a flurry of controversy. See, for example, J. D. Gould, "The Trade Depression of the Early 1620's," *Economic History Review*, 2nd series, VII (1954), 81–90; B. E. Supple, "Thomas Mun and the Commercial Crisis, 1623," *Bulletin of the Institute of Historical Research*, XXVII (1954), 91–94; J. D. Gould, "The Trade Crisis of the early 1620's and English Economic Thought," *Journal of Economic History*, XV (1955), 121–33; and R. W. Hinton, "The Mercantile System in the Time of Thomas Mun," *Economic History Review*,

2nd series, VII (1955), 277–90. But the most sustained discussion of this period is to be found in B. E. Supple, *Commercial Crisis and Change in England, 1600–1642, a Study in the Instability of a Mercantile Economy* (London, 1960).

A general survey of the seventeenth-century trading situation unsympathetic to the notion of mercantilism is to be found in W. S. Hewins, *English Trade and Finance Chiefly in the 17th Century* (London, 1892) while the pattern of the later seventeenth century is discussed by Charles Wilson in *Profit and Power, A Study of England and the Dutch Wars* (London, 1957). See also H. F. Kearney, "The Political Background of English Mercantilism," *Economic History Review,* 2nd series, XI (1959), 484–96.

Aspects of the early eighteenth century are discussed by D. K. Reading, *Anglo-Russian Commercial Treaty of 1734* (New Haven, 1938) and by P. J. Thomas, *Mercantilism and the East India Trade* (London, 1926, reprinted London, 1963), which concentrates on the controversy between the English woollen and silk manufacturers and the East India Company and English calico printers. N. A. Brisco analyzes *The Economic Policy of Robert Walpole* (New York, 1907).

The colonial policy of European powers in the early modern period has often been described as mercantilist, and it appears that all the European colonial powers acted in very much the same way towards their colonies in the sixteenth, seventeenth, and eighteenth centuries. The British case has been most fully described. An easily accessible volume of documents is Merrill Jensen, *English Historical Documents: IX, American Colonial Documents to 1776* (London, 1955). Then there are the writings of the American Imperialist school such as G. L. Beer, *The Old Colonial System, 1660–1754* (New York, 1912, reprinted Gloucester, Mass., 1958), *The Commercial Policy of England towards the American Colonies* (New York, 1893), and *British Colonial Policy, 1754–1765* (New York, 1907); C. M. Andrews, *The Colonial Period of American History* (New Haven, 4 vols., 1934–38); and Lawrence Gipson, *The British Empire before the American Revolution* (New York, 13 vols., 1936–67). In his chapter in the *Cambridge History of the British Empire,* I, ed. J. Holland Rose (London, 1929), J. F. Rees discussed "Mercantilism and the Colonies." More detailed treatments of British colonial policy are to be found in L. A. Harper, *The English Navigation Laws* (New York, 1939), and O. M. Dickerson, *The Navigation Acts and the American Revolution* (Philadelphia, 1951). Articles dealing with this issue include L. A. Harper, "Mercantilism and the American Revolution," and R. B. Morris, "Labor and Mercantilism in the Revolutionary Era," both in *The Era of the American Revolution,* ed. R. B. Morris (New York, 1939); J. Austin Williams, "English Mercantilism and Carolina Naval Stores, 1705–1776," *Journal of Southern History,* I (1935), 169–85; W. A. Williams, "The Age of Mercantilism; an Interpretation of the American Political Economy, 1763–1828," *William and Mary Quarterly,* 3rd series, XV (1958), 419–37; R. A. Plath, "British Mercantilism and British Colonial Land Policy in the Eighteenth Century," *Wisconsin University Summaries of Doctoral Dissertations,* IV (1940), 96–98; and Curtis Nettels, "British Mercantilism and the Economic Development of the Thirteen Colonies," *Journal of Economic History,* XII (1952), 105–14. See also M. Lawson, *Fur: A Study in English Mercantilism, 1700–1775* (Toronto, 1943); and C. R. Haywood, "Mercantilism and Colonial Slave Labor, 1700–63," *Journal of Southern History,* XXIII (1957), 454–64.

Studies in English of mercantilism in other European countries are comparatively sparse. The best introduction is to be found in the pamphlet on *Mercantilism* by Charles Wilson already mentioned, which has a section discussing "The System Elsewhere," in Heckscher's *Mercantilism,* and in the chapter on "Mercantilist and Physiocratic Growth Theory" (and the long appendix to this chapter) by Joseph J. Spengler in *Theories of Economic Growth* (New York, 1960), ed. Bert Hoselitz. Of the French mercantilist writers, notably Jean Bodin (1520–96), Antoine de Montchrétien (1576?–1621), and Richard Cantillon (1680–1734), little has been translated except for Jean Bodin's *The Response of Jean Bodin to the Paradoxes of Malestroit* (Washington, D. C., 1946), which is also included in Monroe (ed.), *Early Economic Thought;* and Richard Cantillon, *Essai sur la nature du commerce en general,* ed. H. Higgs (London, 1931). But the course of French policy and practice in the seventeenth century is discussed by Heckscher, and by C. W. Cole in *Colbert and a Century of French Mercantilism* (New York, 1939, 2 vols.), which incorporated in its first three chapters the same writer's previous volume on *French Mercantilist Doctrines before Colbert* (New York, 1931). This story is continued in C. W. Cole, *French Mercantilism, 1683–1700* (New York, 1943). Together these provide the most detailed examination in English of continental mercantilism. Building on the work of Cole, Louis Rothkrug in *Opposition to Louis XIV, the Political and Social Origins of the French Enlightenment* (Princeton, N. J., 1966) has extended the discussion into the eighteenth century, showing that moral, political, religious, and speculative elements were just as important in the mercantilist scheme of things as the economic. Mercantilist views on the subject provide the jumping-off point for Joseph J. Spengler, *French Predecessors of Malthus, a Study of Eighteenth Century Wage and Population Theory* (New York, 1965). F. C. Palm discussed the *Economic Policies of Richelieu* (Urbana, Ill., 1920), and A. J. Sargent wrote an earlier study of the *Economic Policy of Colbert* (London, 1899). In a review article of Heckscher's *Mercantilism* called "Le Mercantilisme: un état d'esprit," *Annales d'histoire économique et sociale,* 6e année (Mars 1934), pp. 160–3, Marc Bloch argued that the manifestations of mercantilism were to be found in France in small states such as Burgundy as well as in great ones. Two aspects of French mercantilist policy are considered by A. P. Usher in *The History of the Grain Trade in France, 1400–1710* (Cambridge, Mass., 1913) and by Martin Wolfe in "French Views on Wealth and Taxes from the Middle Ages to the Old Regime," *Journal of Economic History,* XXVI (1966), 466–83, which argues that in the field of fiscal policy, mercantilism was a new departure.

Of the leading German mercantilist writers, V. L. von Seckendorff (1626–92), J. H. G. von Justi (1720–71), Joseph Freiherr von Sonnenfels (1733–1817), and Philipp Wilhelm von Hornigk (1638–1712), there is no recent discussion in English, but see Albion W. Small, *The Cameralists, Pioneers of German Social Policy* (Chicago, 1909). A passage from *Österreich über Alles, wann es nur will* (1684) by Philipp Wilhelm von Hornigk is reprinted in Monroe (ed.), *Early Economic Thought.* There has been no thorough English consideration of mercantilist thought and practice in central Europe or in Russia, but Hermann Freudenberger has discussed the role of "Three Mercantilistic Proto-Factories," *Business History Review,* XL (1966), 167–89, in the industrial development of Bohemia, and Arcadius Kahan has examined "A Proposed Mercantilist Code in the Russian Iron Industry, 1734–36," *Explorations in Entrepreneurial History,* 2nd series, II (1965), 75–89.

As far as the Netherlands are concerned, Gustav Schmoller held that the Dutch were from the first the sternest and most warlike of monopolists after the mercantilist fashion that the world has ever seen, whereas Eli Heckscher concluded that they were less affected by mercantilist tendencies than most other countries. But there has been no more recent detailed discussion in English of the history of the Netherlands in the seventeenth and eighteenth centuries from this point of view.

Spanish mercantilism may be studied in W. G. F. Roscher, *The Spanish Colonial*

System (New York, 1904, tr. E. G. Bourne); C. H. Haring, *Trade and Navigation between Spain and the Indies in the Time of the Habsburgs* (Cambridge, Mass., 1918), and *The Spanish Empire in America* (New York, 1947); J. Klein, *The Mesta,, a Study in Spanish Economic History, 1273–1836* (Cambridge, Mass., 1920); R. Herr, *The Eighteenth Century Revolution in Spain* (Princeton, N. J., 1958); and in the essay on "Spanish Mercantilism before 1700" which E. J. Hamilton contributed to *Facts and Factors in Economic History* (Cambridge, Mass., 1932), ed. A. H. Cole and others. On the development of economic thought in Spain from the sixteenth to the eighteenth centuries, see M. Grice-Hutchinson, *The School of Salamanca, Readings in Spanish Monetary Theory, 1544–1605* (London, 1952); B. W. Dempsey, "The Historical Emergence of the Quantity Theory," *Quarterly Journal of Economics,* L (1935), 174–92; R. S. Smith, "The Wealth of Nations in Spain and Hispanic America, 1780–1830," *Journal of Political Economy,* LXV (1957), 104–25; and E. J. Hamilton's summary, "The Mercantilism of Geronimo de Uztariz: a Reexamination (1670–1732)" in *Economics,*

Sociology and the Modern World (Cambridge, Mass., 1935), ed. N. E. Himes, pp. 111–29. One aspect of the breakdown of Spanish mercantilism with respect to the colonies in the eighteenth century is discussed by Harold A. Bierck in "Tobacco Marketing in Venezuela, 1798–1799: An Aspect of Spanish Mercantilistic Revisionism," *Business History Review,* XXXIX (1965), 489–502.

Carlo Cipolla discusses the problems of "The Decline of Italy: The Case of a Fully-Matured Economy," *Economic History Review,* 2nd series, V (1952), 178–87; A. E. Monroe reprints part of the work of Antonio Serra in his *Early Economic Thought.* Otherwise, apart from the discussions in Heckscher, Spengler, and Wilson, Italy is neglected in English discussions of mercantilism.

As with Russia and eastern Europe, the extent of the discussion of Scandinavian economic policy and thought in the sixteenth, seventeenth, and eighteenth centuries has been limited, but see, as before, Heckscher, *Mercantilism,* and also his *Economic History of Sweden* (Cambridge, Mass., 1954).